TRAVELERS' HANDBOOK
BONAIRE

D1377766

TRAVELERS' HANDBOOK
BONAIRE

RIEN VAN DER HELM

ELMAR MEDIA SERVICE BV

BONAIRE TRADING CO LTD NV

The information contained in this book was checked as rigorously as possible before going to press. Guidebook information, however, is notoriously subject to being outdated by changes in telephone numbers and opening hours, and by fluctuating hotel and restaurant standards. While every care has been taken in the preparation of this guide, the author and publishers cannot accept any liability for any consequences arising from the use of information contained herein.

Word of thanks
The author would like to thank his wife Mrs Ellen van der Helm-Piller, Mr Niki Tromp of the Bonaire Tourist Board Office, the Netherlands Antilles National Parks Foundation Bonaire, Mrs Lous Westermann and Koudijs Reizen in Gouda (The Netherlands) for their kind cooperation.

Copyright
All rights reserved. No part of this publication may be reproduced, stored in a retrieval system or transmitted in any form or by any means, electronic, mechanical, photocopying, recording or otherwise, without the prior written permission of the author. Any person who firms any unauthorized act in relation to this publication may be liable to criminal prosecution and civil claims for damages. Brief text quotations are exempted for book review purposes only.

Colophon
Travelers' handbook for Bonaire is a publication of Elmar Media Service b.v., Delftweg 147, 2289 BD Rijswijk, The Netherlands
Distribution: Bonaire Trading Co Ltd. NV
P.O. Box 115, Bonaire, Netherlands Antilles
copyright: Rien van der Helm - MCMLXXXVIII
copyright: Photos: Rien van der Helm
copyright: Underwater photos: Jerry Schnabel, Photo Bonaire (Model: Suzan Swygert)
Maps: Marian Stenchlak
Cover design: Han Janssen
Type-set: DTQP, Schiedam
ISBN 906120 6820

CIP DATA KB

Helm, Rien van der

Travelers' handbook for Bonaire/Rien van der Helm
Rijswijk: Elmar - II, photos, maps - (Elmar travelers' handbooks)
ISBN 90-6120-682-0
SISO 988.9 UDC 917.298.83 (036) NUGI 471
Headwords: Bonaire, travelers' guides

CONTENTS

PREFACE

BON BINI!

Bonaire is the most eastern island of the Leeward Antillean islands. This island, with a modest number of inhabitants, is in no way inferior to its sister islands Aruba and Curaçao. Each of the three ABC-islands has its own character and a corresponding charm. In many ways Bonaire is a unique island. It is unspoiled, quiet, has a very friendly population and a lovely flora and fauna, with underwater scenery of an unprecedented beauty. Reason enough for an enthusiastic scuba diver like me to have given my heart to this charming island. However, Bonaire has much more to offer to the vacationist: a wonderful climate, beautiful sand beaches, excellent restaurants, interesting sights, etc. In short, everything is there to make a vacation on this island an unforgettable event. Apart from practical information about hotels, restaurants and sights, in this travelers' handbook you will also find a short outline of the history of the island, extensive information about its (water)sports possibilities, going out and in particular much, very much information about diving. Bonaire is one of the main diving destinations of the world, and everyone who has been diving there will confirm that the water around Bonaire is a true paradise. For non-divers as well a vacation on Bonaire is worthwhile, because from the water surface snorkelers can too enjoy the splendid and fascinating underwater world. Moreover, this island has a great number of excellent diving schools that will gladly teach you the principles of scuba diving. In this way your vacation may be the beginning of new and fascinating leisure activities. A hobby which is very captivating, as I know from my own experience.

Rien van der Helm

CHAPTER 1

BONAIRE, WHAT KIND OF ISLAND IS THAT?

COUNTRY AND PEOPLE

INTRODUCTION

On 15 December 1954, in the Knights' Hall in The Hague, Queen Juliana signed a treaty, in which the Netherlands gave practically complete autonomy to her last colonies, Surinam and the Netherlands Antilles. This treaty, called Charter for the Kingdom of the Netherlands, was altered on November 25, 1975. On that date Surinam withdrew from the Kingdom of the Netherlands and became a completely independent republic. Since that date the Kingdom of the Netherlands was made up only of the Netherlands and the Netherlands Antilles, consisting of the islands Aruba, Bonaire and Curaçao (also called the ABC-islands), and Saba, St Eustatius and St Maarten (the so-called S-islands). This changed again on the first of January 1986. On that date the so-called Status Aparte became effective for Aruba and for a period of ten years the island received an independent status within the Kingdom of the Netherlands. This Status Aparte was obtained after a long political fight and ratified during a Round Table Conference in March 1983. Therefore at present the Kingdom of the Netherlands is made up of three autonomous territories: the Netherlands, the Netherlands Antilles and Aruba. The islands Bonaire, Curaçao, Saba, St Eustatius and St Maarten have formed the Netherlands Antilles since the first of January 1986.

The name Antilles (derived from the legendary island Antilia, which in the fifteenth century was rumored to be located between Western Europe and Eastern Asia, but which was never found) stands for the group of islands extending from the north-east point of South America to Florida in North America. This group of islands is more or less encompassed by the Gulf of Mexico, the Caribbean Sea and the Atlantic Ocean, and consists of a varied collection of former colonies and current overseas territories, crown colonies and departments of faraway powers. The long-drawn-out chain

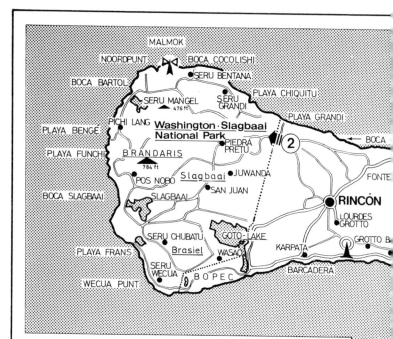

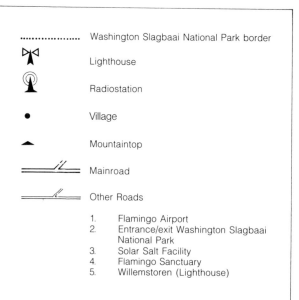

.... Washington Slagbaai National Park border

Lighthouse

Radiostation

• Village

Mountaintop

Mainroad

Other Roads

1. Flamingo Airport
2. Entrance/exit Washington Slagbaai National Park
3. Solar Salt Facility
4. Flamingo Sanctuary
5. Willemstoren (Lighthouse)

BONAIRE

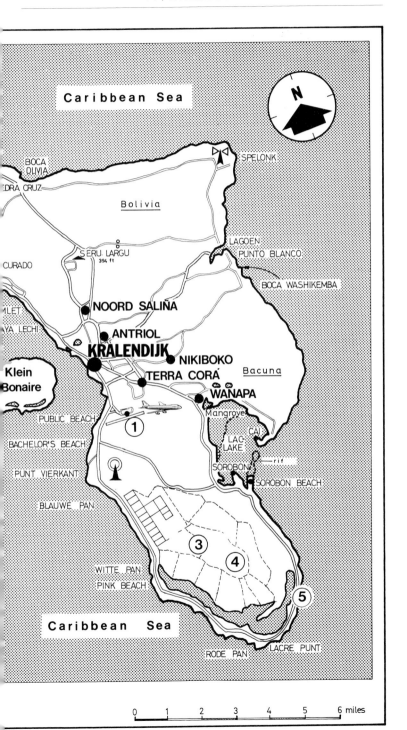

Caribbean Sea

N

BOCA OLIVIA

ORA CRUZ

Bolivia

SPELONK

SERU. LARGU
394 ft

CURADO

LAGOEN
PUNTO BLANCO

BOCA WASHIKEMBA

NOORD SALINA

MLET

YA LECHI

ANTRIOL

KRALENDIJK

NIKIBOKO

TERRA CORÁ

Bacuna

Klein
Bonaire

WANAPA

PUBLIC BEACH

Mangrove

①

CAI

BACHELOR'S BEACH

LAC-
LAKE

SOROBON

rif

PUNT VIERKANT

SOROBON BEACH

BLAUWE PAN

③

④

WITTE PAN

PINK BEACH

⑤

Caribbean Sea

RODE PAN

LACRE PUNT

0   1   2   3   4   5   6 miles

of islands covers about 2,000 miles and is divided into three groups: the Bahama Islands near Florida, the Greater Antilles, including among others the islands Cuba, Haiti and the Dominican Republic (Hispaniola), Jamaica and Puerto Rico, and the Lesser Antilles, including the American Virgin Islands such as St Thomas, the (former) British islands such as St Montserrat, St Lucia, Anguilla, Antigua, the French islands such as Martinique and Guadeloupe, and Aruba and the Netherlands Antilles. Moreover, regarding the Lesser Antilles a distinction is made between the so-called Windward Islands and the Leeward Islands. This appellation originates from the time when there were still only sailing vessels and is based on the location of the islands in relation to the north-east tradewind; this is a strong wind, permanently blowing from the center of the Atlantic Ocean in the direction of the equator. The Dutch islands Saba, St Eustatius and St Maarten (the northern part of which is French territory and is part of the department of Guadeloupe) are north of this north-east tradewind and therefore above the wind, and Aruba, Bonaire and Curaçao are on the southern side and thereforedownwind, close to the South American continent. The distance between the two island groups is roughly 560 miles. Although the Antillean islands bear strong resemblances due to their location and their physical and climatic circumstances, there are big differences as well, mainly because the political situation differs greatly on the individual islands. The British, Portuguese, Spaniards and Dutch conquered many an island in previous centuries and brought about a disintegration that resulted in striking differences in political organization, divergent cultural patterns and a diversity in use of language. Since the seventeenth century the Antillean islands Aruba, Bonaire, Curaçao, Saba, St Eustatius and St Maarten have belonged to the Netherlands. This travelers' handbook focuses on Bonaire, the most eastern island of the Leeward Antilles.

CLIMATE

Bonaire has a tropic-arid climate with as most outstanding features much, very much sun and a nearly constant tradewind. This wind blows with a speed varying from about 12 to sometimes 16 mph and has a very pleasant and cooling effect. The tradewind blows hardest in the month of June and gentlest in November. When an occasional calm occurs, this is mainly in the period August-November. The average annual temperature is about 82°F. There is little difference between daytime temperature and nighttime temperature, and the difference between summer temperature and winter temperature is only 18 degrees. In January and February it is coolest, with daytime temperaturer averaging at least 84°F and a nighttime temperature of about 77°F. In September and October it is warmest, with daytime temperatures averaging 88°F and a nighttime temperature of about 82°F. A day without sunshine is a rarity on Bonaire. The mean annual rainfall is about 22 inches. If rain falls, it is mostly in the morning in the form of brief but heavy local showers. Most of the rain falls in the period October - December. November is by far the wettest month, with an average rainfall of over 28 inches and a minimum of ten rainy days. It should be noted, however, that these figures are average figures over a long period and that there may also occur extremely wet or extremely dry years.

In 1959 for instance, only a little more than 8 inches of rain fell, while in 1950 up to 38 inches of rain came down. Tropical storms and tornados do not occur on Bonaire. All in all, it is dry and sunny almost throughout the year. The temperature of the seawater is hardly different from the temperature of the air and averages 80°F. Because Bonaire is situated close to the equator, the sunsets and -rises are regular.

CULTURE

The culture of the Netherlands Antilles and accordingly also that of Bonaire can to a large extent be compared to that of other Caribbean islands. The historical (colonial) backgrounds of the various islands bear much resemblance and consequently there are also many cultural resemblances. What we find here is a blend of Caribbean, West European and West African influences. Taken together, there are often designated as Creole culture. Regarding the Leeward islands, Latin American influences may be added, in view of the location of the islands close to the South American continent. Important is the development on the Leeward islands of Papiamentu (see further Language), a mixed language in which all influences mentioned above can be traced. The great diversity of inhabitants, varying from Dutchmen to descendants of African plantation slaves, has been decisive in the rise of the current Creole culture. The varied mixture of customs and traditions is not only reflected in the language,

Boy with a hoop and an old Bonairean cottage in the background

but also in typically Antillean music, dance forms and costumes.

In 1948 the Dutch government founded the Foundation for Cultural Cooperation (better known by its Dutch acronym sticusa), with the aim of promoting cultural exchanges between the Netherlands and her Overseas Territories (at the time still including Indonesia and Surinam). In the meantime this aim has been changed into promoting the development of a characteristic Antillean culture and stimulating mutual contacts in the cultural field. Important in this respect are the cultural centers on the various islands. On Bonaire the Cultural Centrum Bonaire was founded in 1956. Its objective is the stimulation of cultural self-activation. It also runs the Central Library, organises various courses and, by arrangement with the Island Government, organises a great number of cultural and folkloristic activities and events (for more information see chapter 6, Folklore).

ECONOMY

Generally speaking the economy of the Netherlands Antilles is based on three pillars: the processing of crude oil, the tourist industry and service. Essentially, this also goes for the economy of Bonaire. Throughout the ages the economic situation of this isle has never been really good. In the period of the West India Company it was against its will turned into a plantation for the benefit of Curaçao. This governmental plantation was never really remunerative and afterwards as well the economic situation of the island was poor. Natural resources of any importance were lacking and the climate and the character of the soil make the island unsuited for agriculture and cattle breeding. The absence of natural resources and an active extensive primary sector has paralyzed the rise of trade. As a result, the economy is still small, with a very lop-sided character. Nowadays the majority of the professional people are employed in the tertiary sector. Agriculture and cattle breeding are negligible as sources of income. Only a very small percentage (not even 0.5%) of the professional population finds work in the primary sector. The fishing industry is especially aimed at the local market and therefore not big. The main sources of income are the salt industry, transshipment of oil, the textile industry and tourism. What follows is a short survey:

For the past few years the salt production on Bonaire has had a stimulating effect on the poor economic situation of the island. The Antilles International Salt Company, a daughter company of the International Salt Company from the United States, has been granted in concession the old

Fischer cleaning his catch near Lac

saltpans near the Salt Lake, and has exploited them since 1966. The salt is extracted by means of the natural process of evaporation. It is then gathered and, by means of a modern conveyor-belt, carried to the shipping-pier, from where it is transported by freighter. The salt export has developed into a quite important pillar of the Bonairean economy. In 1975 the Bonaire Petroleum Corporation N.V. (Bopec), a common daughter of Paktank, Rotterdam, The Netherlands, and Northville Industries, United States, established an oil terminal on Bonaire. In doing so the oil industry made its entry on Bonaire as well. The oil terminal is located on the west coast near the Washington-Slagbaai National Park west of the Goto Lake. Here oil from supertankers coming from Venezuela is stored and subsequently transshipped into smaller tankers carrying the oil to the place of destination (mainly the United States). The establishment of this oil terminal influenced employment in a positive way.

The industrial sector on Bonaire has hardly developed. The textile production is worth mentioning because it is of great importance to the employment - especially of women. Originally set up in 1963 as an employment provision project under the name Cambes Textiles N.V. as a continuation of the Bonaire Confectie Fabriek N.V., the firm manufactures mainly uniforms and industrial clothing for the local market (Aruba and Curaçao).

Compared with Aruba, Curaçao and St Maarten, tourism on Bonaire is still in its infancy, but the island has excellent prospects to develop into a pleasant destination for tourists. It is especially plausible that Bonaire will witness a growing dive tourism: vacationists whose hobby is scuba diving and who wish to practice this sport during their vacation. Bonaire is considered to be one of the three best diving places in the world and more and more divers have discovered this. At this moment the hotel capacity is still limited but there are plans to increase the number of rooms so that more tourists can stay on the island at the same time. In the past few years residence tourism on Bonaire has grown splendidly. Tourism is increasingly developing into one of the most important pillars of the economy of Bonaire.

The greatest employer on the island is the government. More than 75% of the professional population are employed in the service sector. All in all the economy of Bonaire is far from rosy and people will have to put up with the necessary efforts in order to reduce the high unemployment rate (more than 11%). However, one is dependent on third parties for sales, raw materials and capital. As a consequence of the unemployment a considerable part of the (professional) population leaves the island in order to find a job else-where, often on the sister islands Aruba and Curaçao. As a result of this, the active professional population is relatively small.

EDUCATION

On Bonaire there is practically no illiteracy. This is especially the result of the excellent education, which, by Caribbean standards, is of a very high level. In principle everyone, ir-respective of race, religion and origin, is entitled to an education. At the age of four, a child can go to a nursery school and at the age of six, it can go to an elementary school,which lasts six or seven years. Here the child is taught Dutch, reading, writing, arithmetic, geography, history, biology, music, drawing, physical education, traffic education, handicraft, sociology and Papiamentu. Besides, at many schools English and Spanish are taught in the higher grades. The language of instruction is Dutch, which especially in the first years confuses many children. After primary education there is the possibility of secondary education. On Bonaire the highest form of secondary education is Higher General Secondary Education. If people want still higher education they have to go to Curaçao. Apart from advanced elementary education and higher general secondary education, they can choose lower, intermediate or higher vocational education. The next step is going to university. As a rule people are dependent on Curaçao, the Netherlands or the United States for higher and university education. Since the beginning of the 1970s it has been possible to attend some forms of higher education on Curaçao. Since 1979 this island even has a university: the University of the Netherlands Antilles. On 12 January 1979 this was established by a so-called Land's Order. The university owes its existence to a merger of the High School of the Netherlands Antilles and the Antillean College of Advanced Technology on Curaçao. It has a juridical faculty, a faculty of technical science, a faculty of social and economic science and a faculty of medical science. The latter faculty is not active yet; no lecturers have been appointed and consequently it is not yet possible for students to enroll. In cooperation with the medical faculty of the State University of Groningen (The Netherlands) one can study medicine. In this case part of the training takes place in the Sint Elisabeth Gasthuis on Curaçao. Regarding the three other faculties, one can take exams for the 'drs' degree Antillean law, graduate in electrotechnics, architecture, mechanical engineering, civil technics, management science or public administration. There is training at doctoral and bachelor's degree levels. The university has a campus offering room to over 100 students from the other Antillean islands. The university complex was designed by the architect T. Janga. In addition, on Curaçao there are furthermore Teacher Training Colleges for both elementary and secondary schools. Although it is striking that there is no compulsory education, the number of children not going to school on Bonaire is very small!

FLORA AND FAUNA

Land

As a result of the tropic-arid climate with its lack of rain the flora (on the dry soil) of Bonaire is rather poor. It includes about 500 species. There are no evergreens and the vegetation is mainly made up of thorned shrubs such as cacti (see further), agaves (Agave vivipara) and aloe (Aloe barbadensis), and lower types of trees, for instance the Dividivi or Watapana (Caesalpinia coriaria), which is very special because of its wind-determined form. Mangrove vegetation (Conocarpus erectus) occurs especially on the usually claylike soil along inner bays. Furthermore, it is striking that many of the plant species and families found on Bonaire, are represented by one species only and that many of the species can be considered to be weeds. In spite of this, many a beautiful thing can be seen on Bonaire. Especially in the Washington-Slagbaai National Park, the area in the north-east around the highest hill, the Brandaris, a magnificent and in some respects unique flora and fauna is found. As far as the flora is concerned, what is most striking is the great diversity of cacti. This family of plants has the capacity to quickly absorb water after a shower and to store this in the stalk. In dry times it closes completely and lives on the water supply it has built up. Spread over Bonaire a large number of varieties is found. Some common cactus species are: Kadushi (Cereus repandus), a tree-like (and endemic sort!) candle cactus with grey-green branches and oblong red, violet or light green fruit; the Pricklypear (Opuntia wentiana), a disc cactus with grey/white thorns, yellow flowers and red pearlike fruit, Milon di Seru (Melocactus), a bulb cactus with flowers between the white hairs on the top; and the Yatu (Lemaireocereus griseus), a smaller candle cactus, the fruit of which bears thorns and

The typical dividivi or Watapana tree

which has the striking feature that, contrary to the Kadushi, its thorns are regularly grouped in rosette-shape. Important and common tree species on the island are, apart from the Divi-divi mentioned before, among others Dyewood (Haematoxylon brasileto), Lignum vitae (Guaiacum officinale), West-Indian Birch (Bursera simaruba), Palu di sia blanku (Bursera bonairensis), Yellow-wood (Casearia tremula), Calabash (Crescentia cujete) and Palu huku (Jacquinia barbasco). Worth mentioning are furthermore Flamboyant (Delonix regia), Kibrahacha (Tabebuia billberghii) and Acacia (Acacia tortuosa).

Fortunately the fauna is a bit better off, but if you compare it for instance with the fauna of the nearby continent of Venezuela, you will conclude that the fauna of Bonaire is limited as well. Bonaire is especially known for the presence of the Caribbean Flamingo (Phoenicopterus ruber ruber). Spread over the whole island this orange-red colored flamingo is still found in fair numbers. There used to be over thirty nesting grounds in the whole Caribbean. However, as a consequence of advancing civilization this number has decreased to only four! For the flamingos make high demands concerning their breeding places. The soil for instance must not be too hard, but neither too soft to make their cone-shaped nests in: a thick layer of firm mud is most ideal. Important is also the presence in the immediate surroundings of enough food with a high degree of salt and drinking-water. Absolute quiet is a last, not unimportant factor. The Salt Lake on South Bonaire is one of the few breeding places in the world still meeting all these requirements. Bonaire is rightly careful of its flamingo breeding place and everything is being done to let the birds brood in all calm. Therefore the nesting ground in the Salt Lake is closed, and open to no one! Nevertheless, on various other places on the island, mainly near the saltpans in the Washington-Slagbaai National Park, the birds, when looking for food, can be admired from a distance. (For more information see chapter 3 Sights, Flamingos, and Washington-Slagbaai NationalPark). Furthermore unique for the island is the Yellow-winged parrot (Amazona barbadensis rothschildi), also known under its local name Lora. This rare parrot can be recognized by its bright green and yellow head and is unfortunately threatened with extinction. They were and still are taken out of their nests when they are young and sold for much money, because they are a popular cage bird. The reason is that the Lora can easily be taught to 'speak' at a young age. Since 1952 the Lora has been legally protected, but during some extremely dry years (for instance in 1977) their number has decreased considerably. There are still people catching them in order to sell them. Their number is nowadays estimated at about one hundred. They brood from May to August and a nest often contains not more than one or two young. Furthermore, only one type of snake is found on the island: the Silversnake (Leptotyphlops albifrons), a harmless species. Sixteen lizard species are also found, eight of which are indigenous; of these the herbivorous Iguana (Iguana Iguana) is the most well-known. The lizards are harmless and live on insects and plants. The herbivorous Iguana is even considered to be a delicacy and owing to this has decreased strongly in number. Bonaire has a reasonable bird-fauna, which, however, is smaller than that of the nearby Venezuelan mainland. Most of the birds of the over 180 species found on Bonaire, just hibernate there or are on their way to other breeding places. About 50 species brood on the island. Some of these belong to the most beautiful in the world, for instance the Brown-throated Caribbean parakeet Prikichi (Aratinga pertinax xanthogenius), the Yellow oriole (Icterus nigrogularis) and the Chibichibi (on Curaçao called Barica Heel), also called Bananaquit (Coereba flaveola). The Prikichi can immediately be spotted because of its magnificent green color and its loud shrieking. The Chibichibi is the most musical of them all. This singing-bird is often very tame and likes to appear where people are found. Its yellow belly tells you it is a Chibichibi. Part of the bird-fauna is made up of the so-called beach-birds: these birds brood on or near the beach. Apart from the birds mentioned above, the following birds are also found frequently on Bonaire: Blue-tailed Emerald (Chlorostilbon mellisugus) and Ruby-topaz humming-birds (Chrysolampis mosquitos), Sandpipers (Calidris), Black-winged stilts (Himantopus himantopus), Bahama pintails (Anas bahamensis), Black-faced grassquits (Tiaris bicolor), Yellow warblers (Dendroica petechia), Tropical mocking-birds (Mimus gilvus), Common ground dove (Columbigallina passerina), White-fronted dove (Leptotila verreauxi), Eared dove (Zenaida auriculata), Snowy Egret (Egretta thula), Brown pelican (Pelecanus occidentalis), Neotropic cormorant (Phalacrocorax olivaceus), Brown booby (Sula leucogaster), Ruddy turnstone (Arenaria interpres), Pearly-eyed thrasher (Margarops fuscatus), Yellow oriole (Icterus nigrogularis), Scaly-naped pigeon (Columba squamosa), Bare-eyed pigeon (Columba corensis) and ten species of Flycatchers (Tyrannidae), including Big grey flycatchers (Tyrannus dominicensis), Small yellow flycatchers (Sublegatus modestus), Small grey flycatchers (Elaenia martinica). Some bird species are protected by law, among others the Lora, the Yellow oriole and the Bananaquit, or in full on Bonaire: Chibichibi bachi pretu, literally translated 'black coat'. Furthermore, a great many goats (in Papiamentu: Kabritu) are found on the island and a smaller amount of donkeys. Especially the large number of goats running free greatly influences the flora of the island. Goats are known to eat whatever they can get and with their gluttony they destroy the vegetation which is vulnerable as it is. It would be wise to do something about this, in order to better protect the vegetation.

Sea

The sea fauna around Bonaire is not inferior to that of the other parts of the Caribbean. The coral reefs of Bonaire are considered to be among the most beautiful of the world. Contrary to what many people think, coral is made up of living organism and is not just 'rock'. Coral consists of limestone formations, deposited by various groups of animals, for instance moss animals and limestone algae, with in between skeletons of limestone-forming organism such as worms, testacean, sea-eggs and sea-acorns. The living organism of the coral belongs to the coelenterates (Coelenterata). Coral reefs are complex households, in which the inhabitants are mutually dependent. If one of the inhabitants disappears (as a result of damage, for instance), this influences the rest of the coral. Living coral is for the greater part made up of a dead nucleus, with on the outside living folds taking care of further limestone deposits. In these polyps one often finds unicellular algae (Zooxanthellae), which play an important part in the forming of limestone. If there are no algae, then the deposit of limestone is considerably less. Most coral reefs retract their polyps in daytime. At night they are usually wide open in order to catch food, mainly plankton. The coral species with the unicellular algae depend on daylight and are therefore especially found in shallow water. Coral species without algae do not depend on daylight and are subsequently also found on a deeper level. Coral reproduces mainly vegetatively by means of bud-forming or by polyp fission. Sexual reproduction also occurs on a modest scale; out of impregnated eggs larvae come, which settle somewhere and start a new colony. Some types of corals frequently found in the Caribbean Sea around Bonaire are: Stinging coral (Millepora), Scleractinians, Gorgonians, Butterprint Brain (Meandroide) and Red Coral. Not only the coral reefs around Bonaire are of an unprecedented beauty, the fish-fauna is magnificent as well. The sea fauna and flora have clearly benefited from the fact that the government made the coastal area around the island a protected area in 1979, by creating a Bonaire Marine Park (for more information see chapter 3 Sights). As a result of this the waters and everything living there to a depth of 200 feet, are part of the Bonaire Marine Park. Some measures, such as the spear fishing-ban (1971) and the ban on taking coral (1975), have clearly been useful. Also regarding the fish fauna. Nowhere along the coast of the Caribbean area the fish are so numerous and so tame (some sorts can even be fed). Some common fish are: Angelfish (Pomacanthus and Holacanthus), Diodontidae, Barracuda(Sphyraena barracuda), Barbi or Goatfish (Mulloidichthys martinicus and Pseudopeneus maculatus, Brantfes or Scorpionfish (Scorpaenidae), Dradu (Coryphyaena hippurus), Grouper or Hind (Bass, Serranidae, Grunt Haemulon), Sharks (Selachii), Cuttle-fish (Cephalopoda), Kambiou or Amberjack (Seriola dumerili), Karkó (Strombus gigas), Spotted Trunkfish and Honeycomb Cowfish (Lactophyrus and Acanthostracion), Crab-fish (Brachyura), Lobsters (Panulirus argus), Ladronchi or Damselfish (Pomacentridae), Wrasses (Labridae), Muraenes (Muraenidae), Parrot fish (Scaridae), Flat fish (Bothus and Achirus), Rays (Batoidei), Sargassum fish or Frog fish (Antennarius and Histrio), Turtles (Chelonia), Snappers (Lutianidae), Tooth carps (Cyprinodontidae), Durgons (Balistidae), Trumpet fish (Aulostomus maculatus), Flying fish (Exocoetidae), Sea horses or Kabai di Awa (Hippocampus hudsonius or Hippocampus reidi) and Starfish (Asteroidea). Of the above-mentioned fish some may be dangerous. I say 'may be' on purpose, because normally they are harmless, only when touched or attacked by man they can be dangerous. This is the case for instance with Brantfes or 'scorpion fish'. This bottom fish is well camouflaged by its spots and form and is hardly visible, also because it is frequently standing still in the water, waiting for a prey (a passing fish which is swallowed in one gulp). A sting from one of their numerous prickles is very painful (not lethal!), because the cutaneous glands give off a very poisonous pituitary matter. The so-called Spotted Scorpionfish (Scorpaena plumieri) is found most frequently. This fish may have a length varying from 8 to 15 inches. Apart from this Scorpion fish there are other fish that bite when feeling threatened. The Barracuda, for instance, a pike species that can have a length of up to 7 feet, is completely harmless if left alone. These fish are curious and tend to follow swimmers at a distance. If you leave them alone, nothing will happen, however. Barracudas have impressive teeth and halve their prey in one bite. So leave them alone, and Morays too. This snake species has a powerful set of teeth and is extremely strong. They may be over 7 feet long and live in holes in the reef. Some divers like to play with them, which does not necessarily cause problems, provided you are an experienced diver and acquainted with the Moray in question. In all other cases it is wise not to come too close. Very common here are the Spotted Moray (Gymnothorax moringa), having a length of 2 to 4 feet and the Goldentail Moray (Muraena miliaris), having a length of between 1 and 2 feet. A bite from a Moray is not lethal but it is painful and will require a great number of stitches. Finally sharks too are found in these regions, but they do not attack people. The water is so full of food that they avoid people, and in view of the clearness of the water, one can hardly be mistaken. Some shark species found here are the Nurse shark (Ginglymostoma cirratum), Hammerhead (Sphyrna), Tiger shark (Galeocerdo cuvier), Blue and Grey sharks (Carcharhinus). For the rest the fish here are totally harmless. The underwater world around Bonaire is utterly magnificent, and fish such as the Yellowtail Snappers and French Angelfish can be fed easily: an unique experience for every diver or snorkeler. On the island you can buy some excellent-publications (in English) with splendid underwater pictures and extensive information about each fish species. You can also buy plastic-covered maps (among others the Reefcomber's Field Guide), which you can even take with you into the water (for instance on a string), in order to look up on the spot the name of the fish you see. An excellent way to get acquainted quickly with the many beautiful fish here.

For those people who would like to know more about the flora and fauna of Bonaire, I refer to the stinapa, the Foundation National Parks Netherlands Antilles. This foundation was established in 1962 with the aim to protect nature on the islands as much as possible. By means of publications the stinapa tries to make the population (and the tourist) aware of the scenery of the islands. These stinapa publications are available at the bookstores on the island.

FORM OF GOVERNMENT

The Netherlands Antilles form an autonomous part within the Kingdom of the Netherlands and have their own government. This implies that basically it is an independent country looking after its own state affairs, with the exception of Defence and Foreign Affairs. For these two matters the Kingdom of the Netherlands is responsible, and a contingent of marines is permanently stationed on the Antilles. The Netherlands Antilles have appointed a representative, the Minister Plenipotentiary, who represents the islands in the Kingdom Government in the Netherlands. The government of the Netherlands Antilles resides in the capital Willemstad on Curaçao; is consists of a Council of Ministers and a Governor. The Council of Ministers is appointed by the Governor after consultation with the house of representatives, the States of the Netherlands Antilles. Queen Beatrix, as the head of state of the Kingdom of the Netherlands, has appointed this Governor as the representative of the Kingdom of the Netherlands. He is not responsible for the decisions and actions of the Antillean government. The major task of the Governor is seeing to it that no decisions are taken that can harm the unity of the Kingdom or that are incompatible with the regulations of the Royal Constitution or with the international government. The Antillean Council of Ministers is responsible to the house of representatives, the aforementioned States of the Netherlands Antilles. These States are elected directly by the voters for a period of four years. Residents of the islands who have the Dutch nationality and who are at least 18 years old, may vote. There is no compulsory attendance. The States of the Netherlands

Antilles consist of 22 members (Curaçao 14, Bonaire 3, St Maarten 3, Saba 1 and St Eustatius also 1 member). Together with the Governor appointed by the Queen, they form the legislature of the Netherlands Antilles. The members of the States come from the Island Councils. For since 1951 every island has been independent as far as its internal administration matters are concerned, and since that date the islands have each had their own administration consisting of the island council, governing council and an administrator. The island councils (Curaçao 21, Bonaire 9, St Maarten 5, Saba 5, St Eustatius 5 members) are-elected every four years by the island-electorate in general elections.

LANDSCAPE/GEOLOGY

Bonaire is made up of a nucleus of old igneous rock and sedimentary rock, formed more than a hundred million years ago by underseas eruptions and oceanic deposits. About sixty million years ago this thick rock appeared above sea level and subsequently it was surrounded by much younger deposits in the form of coral limestone. The oldest rocks - the solid, originally volcanic igneous rock - can still clearly be seen on the summits of among others the Brandaris and

The road along Goto Lake

Bocá (cove) on the wild northeast side of the island

Juwa. The younger rocks, the coral limestone deposits, are softer and the influence of eroding powers has created large plains. As a result of the rising and falling of the sea level during the glacial periods, limestone terraces were formed, three of which can still be seen more or less clearly.

It is especially the high terrace, which is over two million years old and of which some remains can still be seen near Ceru Grandi, which has been affected by erosion. The middle terrace can still be clearly recognized, just like the low terrace, situated close to the coast, which is about forty thousand years old. Under influence of these geological processes an island has come into existence with in the north-west a very pretty hilly landscape, in the center a terrace landscape and in the south a relatively low and flat landscape. The hilly area is characterized by a chain of summits, of which the Brandaris is the highest with 784 feet. Worth mentioning are furthermore the Yuwana (670 ft), Ceru Largu (607 ft), Hobao (601 ft), La Sana (571 ft), Barón, (539 ft), Curaçao (524.7 ft), Ser'i Kamina (521.4 ft), Ceru Mangel (489.4 ft) and near Washington the Piedra Pretu (341.2 ft). This chain of hills of volcanic origin, is more than 70 million years old and for the greater part made up of basalt rock.

Erosion has created the plain of Slagbaai on the west coast.

To the south of this plain one finds a smaller chain of hills, of which the most important summits are the Ceru Wecua (529.6 ft) and Ceru Wasao (408.9 ft), which stretches out as far as Goto Lake. The latter hill consists of limestone and dolomitized limestone, deposited over 10 million years ago. Near the oldest village of Bonaire, Rincón, one is struck by steep walls, varying in height from 160 to over 330 feet. Here the hilly scenery changes abruptly to limestone terraces, like stairways decreasing in height in northern and eastern direction. Characteristic of this landscape in central Bonaire are the steep, vertical precipices with many caves and bays. The terrace landscape of central Bonaire is made up of a high, middle and low terrace. The high terrace ends at the 455 ft high Kibrá di Montaña, where on the south side it is bounded by a steep wall. The middle terrace runs gradually down to the coast, where it changes into a low terrace. South of the line Kralendijk-Lagoen Bonaire is practically flat; this part of the island is only about six to ten feet above sea level. The extreme south consists of a low terrace with saltpans. Saliñas, or saltpans, can also be found inthe north-west of the island. All these saltpans were formed during the rising and falling of the sea level in the glacial period. The valleys caused by this were later closed by coral deposits, which separated the (salt)lakes from the sea. Under influence of the climate - the high temperature in combination with little rain - a high degree of evaporation created these saltpans, which historically have been of great importance. The ever-lashing sea has created so-called bocas or bays at various places along the coast. These are especially to be found along the north coast and to a lesser degree on the west coast of the island. The best-known are Boca Onima (near the indian drawings) and Boca Slagbaai. Finally fine sand beaches have been formed at various places. At about half a mile offshore west of Bonaire there is a small coral isle, called Klein Bonaire. This isle has an area of 1.500 acres, is not inhabited, and apart from some low shrubs, nothing grows here.

LANGUAGE

Although Dutch is the official language of the Netherlands Antilles, English is the medium of communication on the Windward islands and Papiamentu on the Leeward islands. Papiamentu has developed out of Spanish, Dutch, Portuguese, English, French and some African. The name Papiamentu is derived from the verb papia, which in this lan-

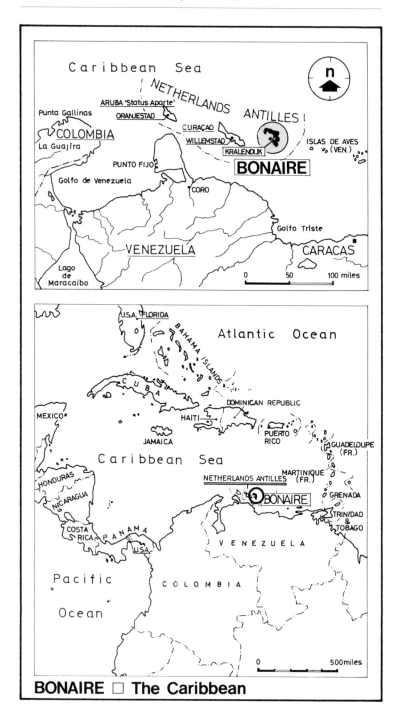

BONAIRE □ The Caribbean

guage means 'to speak'. The language has developed through the ages. Historians and philologists take it that Papiamentu must have originated in the seventeenth century. The basis of Papiamentu is mainly of Portuguese and Spanish origin. However, many people from all over the world were living there, and out of the different languages they spoke - Spanish, Portuguese, Dutch, English, French and African (slaves) - a mixed language originated. The great influence of Spanish and Portuguese may be accounted for by the fact that the Dutch occupied part of Brazil during a period and when they were expelled and fled to these islands, they took with them the Portuguese they had been speaking. Black slaves as well were brought to these islands, taking with them not only African but also Spanish and Portuguese influences, because their masters spoke these languages. The Spanish language was also imported by missionaries doing their work on the islands. With the arrival of the Dutch colonists Dutch was added, and the English and French languages come from occupants of other Caribbean islands in the near vicinity who frequently visited the Dutch islands. The mixed language which developed out of this, has gradually taken the place of a native language. For decades Papiamentu was considered to be a poor and incomplete dialect. However, it was and still is spoken by all social classes (this contrary to other Caribbean mixed languages, which are often spoken exclusively by the lower social classes) and slowly but surely an individual Papiamentu literature has developed. The time that children had to speak exclusively Dutch at school and were not even allowed to speak Papiamentu during the break, is definitely past. Now Papiamentu is the native language of the ABC-islands. There are advanced plans and even experiments to start using Papiamentu as the language of instruction. There is an official spelling of Papiamentu. For that matter, it deviates slightly from the spelling as used on the nearby situated Aruba. It should be noted furthermore that apart from Papiamentu and Dutch, most Antilleans often speak excellent Spanish and English. They have a very good feeling and aptitude for languages.

LOCATION

Bonaire is the most eastern island of the Leeward islands. To be exact, it is located 12°2' and 12°19' north latitude and between 68°11' and 69°25' west longitude. The island is located about 30 miles east of Curaçao, and the distance to the continent of South America (Venezuela) is about 50 miles. The highest point of the island is the hill Brandaris (784 feet), located in the north-western part. Bonaire has a boomerang-like shape. In the bend, the hollow side of which is points south-west, the isle Klein Bonaire can be found at about half a mile off the coast. This coral isle has an area of about 1.500 acres and is not inhabited. The longitudinal axis of Bonaire runs from Lacré Punt in the south to Malmok in the extreme north-west and is over 24 miles. The width varies from 3 to 7 miles. The total surface area of the island is 112 square miles. This makes Bonaire (after Curaçao) the one but largest island of the Netherlands Antilles. The capital of Bonaire is Kralendijk.

NAME

There has been much speculation about the origin of the name of the island. The possible translation from French - good air - is the most obvious explanation, but certainly not the right one. Closer to the truth is the assumption that the name might be derived from the Caribbean word banare, meaning something like 'low land'. To the first Indian inhabitants, coming from the South American continent with its numerous high mountains, Bonaire was of course a relatively low island. The Spaniards, who initially called the island Isla de Palo Brasil, because it abounded with a type of tree called Haematoxylon brasiletto (Dyewood), discovered fairly soon that the Indians had given the island a name. It must have sounded something like Boynay. They adjusted this name to their own spelling and pronunciation, and after the arrival of the Dutch it evolved into the current name. In popular speech the island is now called Boneiru. Recently a new explanation of the origin of the name has been put forward. According to notes of the Jesuit Fray Raymond Pané, who travelled along with the Spaniards, the Indians idolized a raingod and a sungod in the shape of two statues tied together back to back. When it was raining, they prayed on the side of the sungod, and when it was raining the other way around. This Uppergod was called Boy Nay. According to the primitive Indian faith the son of this Uppergod, called Boy Nayil, had the shape of a silver snake. Unlike the other islands in these regions, there are no snakes on Bonaire, except for a harmless silvery kind of snake, which is known to bring good luck. Therefore the Indians called the island Boy Nayre, meaning 'house of the silver snake'. This name is supposed to have been corrupted to the current name through the ages. (Indications for the justness of this assumption can be found in a book by José Juan Arrom, entitled 'Mitologia y Artes Prehisparnica de las Antillas').

POPULATION

Nowadays Bonaire has nearly 11,000 inhabitants. That is very few, compared with the densely populated sister islands Aruba and Curaçao, and if one looks at the size of the island. The history of the island (see chapter 2 History) has to a large extent determined the composition of the current population. An important feature of the population of Bonaire is the ethnic diversity, although the negroid element is most prominent. The original inhabitants were Caiquetio Indians, a primitive people descending from the Arawak Indians, who originally had their residential area in the northern part of South America. At the time of the 'discovery' of Bonaire by the Spaniards (about 1499), these Indians were still living in the Stone Age. In the eyes of the Spaniards the island was of no value at all, and in 1513 they decided that Bonaire, Aruba and Curaçao were Islas Inútiles, in other words: useless islands. Subsequently, in 1515 the Spaniards carried off the whole Indian population of the three islands to employ them as slaves in the copper mines of Santo Domingo on the island Hispaniola (the present-day Dominican Republic and Haiti). A few years later the Spaniard Juan de Ampués managed to have part of the original inhabitants return to the islands. In all he brought back about 200 original inhabitants, so Bonaire was inhabited again, be it on a modest scale. At the same time he tried to interest Indians from the continent to settle on the islands. When the Dutch conquered Bonaire from the Spaniards in 1636, the island was inhabited by a handful of Spaniards and Indians. However, these all fled from the new occupant and Bonaire was depopulated once more. Subsequently, the Dutch turned the island into a plantation for the benefit of Curaçao. For this purpose large numbers of black slaves from Africa were brought to the island. For years on end the population of Bonaire consisted of some hundreds of black slaves and a handful of Dutch who were in charge. For a long time the Dutch authorities prohibited the settlement of (white Dutch) colonists on the island. Nevertheless, some whites settled illegally on the island and Indians from the continent frequently came to Bonaire. However, gradually the Indian part of the population decreased and around 1810 the last fullblood Indians left for the continent, not to return again.

When the order prohibiting residence was lifted at the end of the eighteenth century, the number of whites increased further. However, the negroid part of the population of the island grew much faster and by the middle of the nineteenth century Bonaire had about 800 black slaves and only some tens of whites. With the abolition of slavery in 1862 part of the freed negro population left for other islands. At the beginning of the 20th century the population of Bonaire consisted of over 5,000 souls, the vast majority of which was negroid with only few whites. Of course throughout the ages mulattos, descendants of mixed parents, were added. The population increased to about 7,000 people in the 1920s, to decrease again to about 5,000 in the 1950s. This was caused by the poor economic situation of the island and the rise of the oil industry on Aruba and Curaçao. A lot of unemployed Bonaireans found jobs in the growing oil industry on these islands. After the fifties, the demand for manpower decreased as a consequence of automation and many Bonaireans returned to their native island, which resulted again in a strong increase of the population. In 1980 the island numbered about 8,500 inhabitants and at present this number has increased to approximately 10,400. The majority, over ninety-three per cent, of the inhabitants are of Dutch Antillean origin. Among these are inhabitants that originally came from Aruba, Curaçao and the Windward Antillean Islands. About 90% were born on the island. Furthermore the island has some hundreds of inhabitants coming from the Netherlands, America and Venezuela. A very small percentage comes from other Caribbean islands, such as the Dominican Republic. Another striking feature of the current composition of the population is that the average age (29,6) is under thirty years and that the number of women exceeds the number of men.

RELIGION

The Dutch colonists on Bonaire were nearly without exception Protestant. However, they hardly mixed with the local population, and mission work was left to the missionaries. The Catholic missionaries were considerably more active than their Protestant colleagues, as a result of which a vast majority of the population became Roman Catholic. At present about ninety per cent of the population is Roman Catholic. There are Catholic churches in Kralendijk, the St Bernardus Church (1948), in Rincón, the St Ludovicus Bertrandus Church (1908), and in Antriol we find the Lady of

Coromoto Church (1955).
The number of Protestants is very small. In 1847 a Protestant church was built in Kralendijk and in Rincón as well there is a small Protestant church, built in 1932. Only in 1861 the first Protestant preacher settled on the island. After 1920 other religious groups settled on the island, including the Seventh Day Adventists (1925), the Evangelical Alliance Mission (1952) and the Jehovah's Witnesses (1951). These believers as well built a number of churches. Striking is the absence of Jews, who on the nearby Curaçao, for instance, are prominently present.

Catholic church in Kralendijk

CHAPTER 2

HISTORY

Legend has it that Bonaire was discovered in 1499 by the Spaniard Alonso de Ojeda. In the month of May of that year this commander of noble origin left Spain with a small squad -ron of ships, headed for the Caribbean area. He had been in these areas before when, in his capacity of Captain, he accompanied admiral Christopher Columbus on his second trip to the New World. Already in 1493 Columbus had discovered the Windward Islands. Columbus had managed to gain the exclusive rights for exploratory expeditions of this kind. However, after a good many mutual conflicts, in 1495 the Spanish Queen Isabella deprived him of these rights. Under certain conditions other prominent Spaniards were now also allowed to undertake voyages of discovery. Because of his influential family and because he was on a good footing with Queen Isabella, Alonso de Ojeda was one of the first who obtained permission to undertake such an expedition. Early May 1499 he left from the port of Santa Maria in Spain with a handful of ships, in the direction of the New World. Some two months after his departure, late June 1499, he discovered Curaçao and a neighboring island. On the basis of map drawings and writings historians assume that , apart form Curaçao, he also set foot ashore on Bonaire, but that, on the other hand, he never was on nearby Aruba. Aruba was 'discovered' a few years later during reconnoitering expeditions and, without too much fuss, added to the Spanish territory. At the time of their discovery, the islands, and so Bonaire as well, were inhabited by Caiquetio Indians, primitive and peace-loving people descending from the Arawak Indians, who had their residential area in the northern part of South America. Since the moment that Alonso de Ojeda set foot ashore documents have been written, from which the history of Bonaire, wrapped in darkness until that moment, can be deduced. On his expedition De Ojeda was accompanied by Amerigo Vespucci, Bartolomé Roldán, the cartographer Juan de la Cosa, and others. The latter made the very first map of the Caribbean area. On this map Bonaire is called Isla do Brasil or 'Island of Dyewood'. This name can be explained by the fact that in that time the island abounded with this kind of wood. Later the Spaniards changed the name, after finding out that the autochthonous population called the island differently. The phonetic spelling of their name was Boynay. This name is found on a map by Visconte de Maiollo in 1519. In their writings the Spaniards called the Leeward Islands Islas de los Gigantes (Giants' Islands), because the Indian people were much taller than they. In a letter to his friend Piero de Tomasso Soderini in Florence, Amerigo Vespucci does not only call the Indians tall, but also friendly. They chewed leaves and around their necks they wore two scooped-out calabashes, one containing the leaves and the other a whitish powder. In his letter Vespucci described how with their saliva the Indians wet a wooden stick, which they the put into the white powder and next into their mouth to manipulate the leaves. Vespucci supposed they did this to quench their thirst, but nowadays researchers assume it was probably a light drug. Vespucci visited this island in 1499. The discoverer Alonsode Ojeda had left in the meantime. After his discovery he soon set sail along the coast of Venezuela and then returned to Spain. He never visited the islands again. Some historians even claim that Alonso de Ojeda never was on the islands at all and that it was Amerigo Vespucci who discovered them. The ships of Vespucci and De Ojeda seem to have lost each other during the crossing and when in September Vespucci reached Bonaire and Curaçao, Alonso de Ojeda had already arrived at Santo Domingo. Therefore it is not 100% sure who discovered the islands, but the discovery of the Leeward islands is attributed to Alonso de Ojeda and not to Amerigo Vespucci, after whom America was named!

Original inhabitants

Very little is known about the original inhabitants of the islands before the Spaniards arrived. Excavations have shown that Bonaire was inhabited for hundreds of years prior to the discovery by the Spaniards. This has been concluded from the fact that human remains and traces were found at archaeological excavations on some places on the island. The original islanders (and also the inhabitants of the other Caribbean islands and those of North and South America) are collectively referred to as Indians. This name was given to them by Christopher Columbus, when in 1492 he was the first person to discover the continent on the other side of the Atlantic Ocean. A strange name indeed, but it can be explained as follows: Columbus assumed he had been sailing half the world and that he had arrived at islands that were part of China and the Indies. He did not realize he had arrived at a continent unknown to Europe at the time. The name 'Los Indios' for the Indies is therefore wrong. When people later realized that Columbus had discovered a New World that had no connection at all with the Indies, and that the name was not correct, they did not take the trouble to correct the mistake. Consequently, the local population has always been called 'Indians'.

The number of archaeological sites on Bonaire is small. The main spots are located north of the lagoon Lac and northeast of Kralendijk. All archaeological researches have shown that already a thousand years ago - so over 500 years before the Spanish discovery - the three Leeward Islands were inhabited by Indians who had the same culture as the inhabitants of the South American continent. This was concluded after the close study and comparison of archaeological findings. It has become clear that the Indians who were living on the islands before the Spanish discovery, manufactured the same utensils and lived and worked in the same way as their contemporaries on the mainland of Venezuela. Especially with the Indians who lived in Falcòn and Paraguaná in Venezuela the original islanders bear remarkable resemblances. This region of the Venezuelan mainland is separated from Bonaire by a narrow strip of water that is approximately 50 miles wide. The Indian inhabitants of Bonaire are supposed to have been peaceful and gentle people. It is not known how many Indians lived on the island through the ages. It is assumed that their number varied strongly, but probably there were never more than a few hundred at the same time. Newcomers settled on freespots and due to circumstances people occasionally changed their residence. When the Spaniards came, the Indians were still living in the Stone Age. They lived in small groups, spread over the island, in simple mud huts with only one opening serving as entrance. At various places (including Onima, Ceru Pungi, Ceru Crita-Cabai and in the caves of Spelonk), all over the island Indian cave drawings have been found. The meaning of these drawings is not clear; there are no writings, so one supposes they had a deeper, religious meaning for the Indians. Presumably they fulfilled an important part in sacrificial services and the like. The drawings have never been 'deciphered'. The Indians were extremely primitive and did not engage in agriculture or cattle breeding. They lived from day to day, depending on what fishing yielded and what vegetable food they managed to find. The ancestors of these Indians originally lived in the jungles (on the mainland of Venezuela) and they had some primitive forms of agriculture. However, the Indians on the Leeward Islands were mainly dependent on fishing, and quickly adjusted to the local situation.

The Spanish Period

Because there are no written documents, there is hardly anything to tell with certainty about the history of Bonaire prior to the Spanish conquest. However, there are documents from the period following the Spanish conquest and from these one can learn what happened to Bonaire and its inhabitants. The few early documents show that Bonaire soon was of no use at all to the Spaniards. Following the drastic depopulation of 1515, things were none too bright for the local inhabitants. Only a handful of Indians, for the greater part old or sick people who could not be employed as slaves, formed the total population of Bonaire. This changed in 1526. In that year Juan de Ampués was appointed commander of the three Leeward Islands. He had gotten to know the island population during his stay on Hispaniola, and tried to repatriate these people. In all, he brought back about 200 original inhabitants to Curaçao, and Bonaire too was populated again on a modest scale. Moreover, he tried to interest Indians from the continent in settling on the islands. In spite of this, the three islands still had hardly any value in the eyes of the Spaniards. No gold was found there (in the case of Aruba a misunderstanding, because gold was discovered there in 1824), and neither were the islands suited for agriculture, contrary to many other Caribbean islands. The Spaniards thought the islands only fit to serve as a cattle breeding colony. For this purpose they transported cattle from Europe: sheep, goats, donkeys, cows, pigs and horses. By the way, one should not idealize the cattle breeding of that period: the animals were simply running free and had to fend for themselves. Most animals were not kept for the meat but for the hides. The islands had turned into a kind of farm. Because otherwise they were of no interest to them, the number of Spaniards living there was minimal. Most of them - sixty - were found on Bonaire, because unwanted persons were banned to this island from Venezuela, which was under Spanish control as well. On Curaçao - the largest and main island - one found only ahand ful of Spaniards and consequently it took the Dutch under the leadership of Johan van Walbeeck in 1634 hardly any trouble to conquer this island from the Spaniards.

West India Company

The islands Aruba, Bonaire and Curaçao were of little use to the Spaniards, so the garrisons on the islands were very small. They would have remained Spanish territory until to-day, if by coincidence the Dutch had not taken an interest in them. In those times the Dutch were an undertaking people, sailing all the oceans. They were expert merchants. For their herring-fishery they needed salt. They got this in Spain and Portugal, until the Spaniards and the Portuguese decided to stop supplying the Dutch. Then they were forced to look for new saltpans. These were found in the Caribbean area (on the island St Maarten, for instance). A lively traffic arose between the Netherlands and the Caribbean area. The islands Curaçao and Bonaire were also frequented by ships of the West India Company, founded in 1621. Fresh water was taken aboard or wood was cut to repair the boats, and so on. From the writings of the West India Company we know for instance that Bonaire was frequently visited by Jan Jaricks in 1623, and that in that year admiral Boudewijn Hendricksz organized a festive Easter banquet for his crew there. As far as food was concerned, during their long voyages the sailors depended on dry meat (many years old sometimes), so the stray goats and sheep were a treat to them. The few Spaniards living there at the time did not mind, because they kept the animals only for the hides. When he left, by the way, admiral Hendricksz left his Spanish and Portuguese prisoners behind on the island: about ten persons he had captured during an attack on Punta de Araya in Venezuela. These settled down on the spot that is now Antriol. This place is not situated along the coast but inland, and the name is supposed to stem from the words 'al interior' or 'inside'. Antriol is not the oldest place of Bonaire; that is Rincón. This spot was chosen by the Spaniards because of its ideal location. The first Spaniards settled here in the beginning of the sixteenth century because it was much safer to live inland and because the surroundings had a luxuriant vegetation. The most important factor, however, was safety: from the sea Rincón cannot be seen and possible pirates and other riffraff had to go a long way first, before they could reach the settlement.

The Dutch

So the Dutch had been quite at home in the Caribbean area, and long before there were plans to conquer the Leeward Islands they frequently came to anchor there. The Eighty Years' War (1568-1648) was still raging, so the relation with the Spaniards was far from good. In 1633 the

Dutch had lost an important foothold in the Caribbean area, the island of St Maarten, to the Spaniards. Since the interests in South America (especially in present-day Brazil) were increasing, a base in the Caribbean area was of great importance. The limited number of the Spanish occupants on Curaçao and the other two islands was known, and in April 1634 the West India Company decided to conquer Curaçao -the largest and most important island of the Leeward Islands - in order to obtain a strategic foothold again. A squadron consisting of six vessels, including the flagship Groot Hoorn and the sailing vessels the Eenhoorn and the Brack, left for the West early May 1634, under the command of Johan van Walbeeck and Pierre Le Grand. On 24 June they arrived at St Vincent in the east Antilles, where refreshments were taken in. In the beginning of July the squadron arrived at Bonaire, where they dropped anchor in order to concoct a plan of campaign. The strategy they decided on was simple: they would sail into the harbor of Curaçao and conquer the island. Something went wrong, however. Jan Jansz Otzen, a colored Dutchman, who had pointed out the islands to the West India Company and who knew the local situation, had come along in order to pilot the ships into the harbor of Curaçao. He made a mistake, however, in spite of the fact that the entrance of the Schottegat had been indicated by a big cross. The fleet missed the entrance and was forced to sail on, returning to Bonaire after crossing to Hispaniola. Back in Bonaire the vessel Coninck David joined the fleet. This Dutch ship happened to be in the area and wanted to be present at the conquest. A second effort was made and on 29 July the Dutch navy with the flagship Groot Hoorn bringing up the rear entered the harbor of Curaçao. One can hardly speak of a real conquest, because the resistance of the handful of Spaniards was not worth mentioning. They burnt down the village of Santa Anna, put some wells out of order and then fled to the western part of the island, from where they offered some resistance during a few months.

Nevertheless, the situation became untenable for the Spaniards and on 21 August 1634 they capitulated. The Spaniards had surrendered on the condition that they would be allowed to safely leave the island, a condition that was amply fulfilled by Van Walbeeck. Not only the Spaniards, 32 in all, but also many of their Indian servants (402 persons) whom Van Walbeeck did not trust, were evacuated and not allowed to take with them more than the clothes they wore. From that moment on Curaçao belonged to the Dutch. The island was used as a port for surprise attacks during the

Eighty Years' War. From there the Dutch could harass the Spanish navy. Only two years later, in March 1636, they also took the other two islands Bonaire and Aruba. This was done out of sheer necessity, in order to prevent attacks from these nearby islands. On Aruba some Indians were found, as well as some Spaniards. These left and Aruba was depopulated again. The few Indians still living on Bonaire fled from the new occupant. They took part of their cattle with them and killed the rest. So Bonaire as well was uninhabited by the end of that year.

Agricultural Colony

However, this did not last long, for the active West India Company was busy developing Curaçao into an agricultural colony, and soon Aruba ánd Bonaire were included in these plans. It was the intention to develop Aruba and Bonaire for the benefit of Curaçao. On this island cattle breeding was taken up again, but this time not for the hides as in the days of the Spaniards, but for food for the Dutch inhabitants of Curaçao. On Aruba they started breeding horses, and on Bonaire the winning of salt and dyewood, cattle breeding and the cultivation of maize were (further) developed. To the Dutch Curaçao was not only an important foothold in the war against the Spaniards and Portuguese, but because of its excellent natural harbor - Het Schottegat - it soon developed into an important center of trade as well. Bonaire, on the other hand, became less and less important. At first the island was a not unimportant military foothold, judging by the fort the Dutch built in 1639, with its four guns (which was quite something in those days). Also as far as supplying food for the Dutch garrisons on Curaçao was concerned, Bonaire played an important part. However, after the end of the Eighty Years' War in 1648 it had served its turn as a military foothold; from then on it was only a governmental plantation for the benefit of Curaçao.

Slave trade

After the end of the Eighty Years' War, Curaçao on the other hand became more and more important as a center of trade. At the time Peter Stuyvesant was commander of the islands. Since 1646 he had also been director-general of Nieuw-Nederland, and during a period of 17 years he ruled the Caribbean possessions from there. His administration was of little importance to the Leeward Islands. As administrator of Nieuw-Nederland, present-day New York, he has a prominent place in the history books. Especially in the period 1660-1700 trading on Curaçao flourished as never be-

Slave huts

fore. However, slaves were the main commodity. A black
page in history, but a page that has been decisive in the
further development of the islands. Already in the beginning
of the seventeenth century black slaves were brought from
Africa to the West. This pernicious slave trade was introduced by the Spaniards and the Portuguese. The Spaniards
had a chronic lack of manpower for their (sugar cane) plantations in Brazil. The local Indian people were not suited,
and the Spaniards were compelled to acquire their manpower elsewhere. For this purpose they even made a special contract with the Portuguese, who arranged the supply.
As the Dutch had no plantation colonies initially, they were
not engaged in these practices. However, the colony Nieuw
Nederland and the conquest of Pernambuco in 1629 in
north-east Brazil changed this. In these Dutch colonies
there was also a shortage of workers, so the West India
Company too decided to start transporting slaves. A lively
trade arose between Africa, Brazil and the Netherlands, the
merchandise on the route from Africa to Brazil consisting of
black slaves. In the period from 1637 to 1645 as many as
twenty thousand slaves were brought from Africa to Brazil.
After the peace with Spain in 1648 and the loss of Brazil in
1654, Curaçao developed into the most important center of
the slave trade in the Caribbean area. Especially in the period 1685-1713 the slave trade 'flourished' as never before.

Curaçao had become an open slave market, where merchants from all sorts of nations came to buy slaves. On Bonaire the salt production flourished, and more and more black slaves were employed on the island in order to extract the salt from the saltpans near the present-day Salt Lake (near Blauwe Pan): on bare feet and with their bare hands they gathered and piled up the salt, which was then taken away by boat. Apart from black slaves also convicted Indians and persons who had been punished otherwise were employed in the saltpans. Because of this, Bonaire got the status of a convict colony. Every Monday early in the morning the slaves and convicted marched from their houses in Rincón to the saltpans where they stayed until Saturday. The walk from Rincón to the saltpans took about seven hours. At night they slept in simple mud huts with leaves for a roof. By the middle of the nineteenth century these simple mud huts were replaced by slave huts made of stone. These can still be seen and it is obvious that these small stone houses - with roofs reaching to the waist - cannot be called really commodious. On the contrary, life was hell there; during the day one worked under a burning sun, standing with bare feet in the salt water and the eyes screwed up against the bright sunlight reflected in the salt crystals, and at night one slept in huts that were much too small. It was not called the 'white hell' by coincidence.

Abolition
After 1713 the Dutch slave trade went downhill, partly as a result of increasing English competition. Slowly but surely, slave trade on Curaçao decreased and legend has it that the last ship carrying slaves arrived at Curaçao in 1788. Resistance against the slave trade had increased, and by the end of the eighteenth century committees were set up in various countries with the aim of abolishing the slave trade. In England and the United States this took place in 1808, the Netherlands followed in 1814, France in 1816, and Spain and Portugal forbade their subjects to go on transporting slaves. In 1818 the Netherlands signed a treaty with England to fight the slave trade. Subsequently, in 1821 importing slaves into the colonies was forbidden. However, exports went on until the middle of the nineteenth century. The end of the slave trade, however, did not imply complete abolition. But it was obvious after the slave trade had come to an end that it would only be a matter of time before there would be no more slavery. Also because of the great distance between the colonies and the homeland, The Netherlands, the abolition of slavery was not a big issue

to the Dutch. This was different in the case of the English, for instance, who wanted to abolish slavery for Christian and humanitarian reasons.

Around 1840 also in the Netherlands a movement arose (under the influence of the English), with the aim of abolishing slavery. However, several abolition attempts were in vain, due to economic reasons. Sill, the result was a revision of the so-called slave regulations, as well as better clothing, food and housing. At the same time control on (corporal) punishments was introduced.

Plantation

At the end of the seventeenth century Bonaire was a plantation of the West India Company. A commander and a handful of soldiers, plus a factor keeping an eye on the plantation and the approximately 100 company slaves, were the only representatives of the West India Company. Occasionally Indians of the nearby Venezuelan mainland came to the island to breed horses, but after 1800 these brief visits came to an end. The visiting Indians, however, were left alone and not turned into slaves. During the period of the West India Company, the Dutch nor other white people were allowed to settle on Aruba or Bonaire. Except for the commander and his immediate assistants, initially there were no whites on Bonaire. Despite the ban of the West India

Abandoned country house

Company, small groups of whites settled on the island from time to time. Mercenaries and soldiers whose contracts expired stayed on, because they had gotten married to Indian or black women, and as the power of the Company decreased - late 1791 the West India Company ceased to exist - more and more whites settled on the island. The number of colored people, however, remained much and much larger. In this way the number of black slaves gradually increased, and around 1825 there were over 300 so-called government's slaves on Bonaire. After the fall of the West India Company the slaves had been claimed by the Netherlands, and they were now called government's slaves, or in Papiamentu Catibu di Rei or 'the king's slaves'. The slaves, however, were in poor health and resistance on the island increased. In 1835 a slave called Bintura escaped, and the local government - afraid of a revolt - took drastic measures. The slaves had to leave Rincón and were housed in a special slave village near Terá Cora (Papiamentu for 'red soil'), close to the saltpans. Bintura was captured and imprisoned, but he escaped again and returned home. A big slave revolt, as on Curaçao, never took place on Bonaire.

During the nineteenth century a new population group developed on Bonaire, consisting of redeemed or released slaves. As a reward for special services or for a large amount of money, slaves could gain their freedom. Because the government allowed them to carry on some agriculture on a small plot of land and to sell their products, the slaves could save the required amount of money to buy their freedom. Some of them succeeded in this, which resulted in a completely new population group on Bonaire.

They were, however, obliged to render some services to the government, such as catching slaughter-goats and sheep running free (an American visiting the island in the eighteenth century jokingly called it 'goat island' because so many goats were running free). The goats and sheep mainly grazed in the north and west of the island. They were driven to Slagbaai and then slaughtered. Every week a ship came from Curaçao to fetch the meat. The name Slagbaai (Slaughtering Bay) has been derived from this. Most of the free groups of population were obliged to assist in gathering the animals that were running free. Nevertheless, the Indian population became smaller and smaller. Around 1810 the last fullblood Indians left for the continent and did not return.

English rule
Due to the fact that by the end of the eighteenth century

the Netherlands got mixed up in various wars, including the Austrian War of Succession and the Seven Years' War, things changed on Bonaire as well. In 1795 the Batavian Republic was formed after the French invasion in the Netherlands. Stadtholder Prince WillemV had fled to England and from there he decreed the English to be admitted to the Dutch colonies. The French wanted to prevent an English occupation, and in September 1800 attacked Curaçao. In the thick of the fight an English warship appeared before the harbor, and with both hands the Dutch forces seized this opportunity: they placed the islands under English protection. During this period there were no contacts between Curaçao and Bonaire. After the peace of Amiens in 1802 the English returned the islands to the Batavian Republic and things were as before again. However, peace was of short duration. In Europe France and England entered war again in 1803, and by the end of January 1804 the English attacked Curaçao once more. The attack was repelled, and after a month the enemy withdrew. In 1805 the English attacked again, but due to the assistance of the Venezuelan freedom fighter Luis Brion they were repelled again. Still, it was all going to be in vain, because to the surprise of everyone in the early morning of 1 January 1807 four English ships came sailing into the St Annabaai of Curaçao. There was little resistance and the English took the island. Bonaire as well came under English rule again. The English appointed a commandant on Bonaire, but they did not know what to do with the island, and after 1810 they even leased it in its entirety to some private persons. After some failures it was the shipowner Joseph Foulke, coming from North America and living on Curaçao, who got the island on lease. He went ahead energetically: a great number of trees was cut down (especially guaiacum and Brazilwood or dyewood were popular), and when Bonaire and the other two islands were returned to the Netherlands during the Convention of London in 1816, a great part of the original forests of the island had been destroyed. The whole island was close to becoming a barren plain. At that moment more than 1,100 people were living on the island, including over 400 slaves. During the English rule a large number of white traders had settled on the island illegally. They built their homes around the natural harbor and about 1810 Playa, what is now Kralendijk, was founded. Here was also located the small Fort Oranje, that had to protect the island against invaders. The fort, which had been built at the end of the eighteenth century, housed the Commander until 1837. Afterwards for a long time it served as a depot for govern-

Bust of Luis Brion

ment's goods, and it even was a prison for a while. Around 1868 a wooden lighthouse was built in the fort, which was replaced by a stone beacon in 1932.

Emancipation regulation

After the island had been returned to the Dutch in 1816, it kept the status of government's plantation till 1868. For this purpose over 150 sheep were imported and even a few cows. The exploitation of the island was taken up with new zest and in spite of the order prohibiting residence on the island - which would only be lifted officially in 1868 - again

Fort Oranje

some new inhabitants came from elsewhere. Slowly but surely Playa developed into a small town: various houses were built, including the house of the Governor. About 1840 the name Kralendijk came into use. This name is connected with the spot on which the town was built, for it is located on a dyke of coral rock. At the beginning of the nineteenth century the island had a great many saltpans and exploiting these was very remunerative. New saltpans were laid out and in 1837 four colored obelisks were erected near the Salt Lake to guide the ships coming to fetch the salt. The obelisks were painted red, white, blue and orange (the colors of the Dutch flag and the Royal House). Close to the most southern saltpans - called Red Pan - there was a tall flagpole, on which a red, white, blue or orange flag was hoisted to point out to the ships where they had to be: at Red Pan, Blue Pan, White Pan or Orange Pan. From sea the colored obelisks were clearly to be seen and the ships could come to anchor close to each obelisk. As a result of the steady growth of the salt exploitation, the number of slaves rose gradually, and by the middle of the nineteenth century there were nearly 800 black slaves on Bonaire. In the meantime people in the Netherlands were trying to find out how to give the slaves their freedom, without doing too much economic harm to the plantation owners. On 30 September 1862 the moment had come: on that day the so-called Emancipation Regulation was proclaimed on Curaçao. In all, 6,751 slaves were freed on Curaçao. As a compensation the owners received an amount varying from H*f*l. 30.- to H*f*l. 200.- per slave. On Bonaire 607 government's slaves and 151 private slaves were released. A lot of free slaves left the island to return again shortly afterwards. They settled mainly in and around Rincón and this small village soon developed into a city which was rather big by Bonairean standards.

Allotment

The abolition of slavery also put an end to the government's exploitation of the island, and it was soon decided to lot out the government's lands and to sell them by public auction. In 1867 the wood and cattle breeding lots - five altogether - were sold for the small amount of H*f*l. 84,000.- to J.F. Neuman Czn. & Co. and E.B.F. Hellmund. The nine salt lots remained unsold initially, but in 1870 E.B.F. Hellmund also became the owner of the saltpans of Bonaire for H*f*l. 150,000.-. All this meant that the whole island population was now dependent on two large landowners, which had its disadvantages. At the time the population of Bonaire consisted of former slaves, small farmers and cattle breeders, who were now confronted with such matters as the abolition of communal grazing rights, truck system and very low wages. Poverty reigned and the two large landowners also hit badly when the government made a new law, levying 10% taxes on the export of charcoal, resin, cattle and salt. The poor economic situation made many inhabitants of the island leave for Venezuela at the turn of the century, where they found jobs in the copper mines. For those who stayed behind on Bonaire, life was poor. The First World War did not affect Bonaire and while on both sister islands the black gold - the oil industry - brought the economy to unprecedented heights, the economic situation and standard of living on Bonaire did not come up to expectations. The rise of the oil industry on Aruba and Curaçao had a positive effect on Bonaire as well. The economy of the Neth erlands Antilles advanced by leaps and bounds due to the oil and the employment it entailed, and money was made available to allow Bonaire also to benefit from the profits made. Roads were improved and blacktopped, the landing stage in the harbor was renewed, electricity and telephone

The beautifully restored Passanggrahan in Kralendijk

Fisher offering his ware in the fish market

Memorial to those who fell in the Second World War

connections were installed, lighthouses built and medical provisions improved. Important was also the construction of an airport. On 30 May 1936 for the first time a plane coming from the sister island Curaçao landed on the island.

Internment Camp
While the First World War did not influence daily life on Bonaire, the Second World War clearly left its traces. On 10 May 1940, 461 persons were transported to Bonaire and confined in a so-called internment camp consisting of wooden shacks. They were Germans and pro-German Dutchmen (members of the National Socialist Movement), considered to be dangerous to the state on the other islands. As a result, things were livening up, and Bonaire was frequented by soldiers and officers. In 1944 Princess Juliana visited the island, a few weeks later followed by Eleanor Roosevelt, the American First Lady. Unconsciously a first

step towards a new source of income - tourism - had been made. For the purpose-built wooden internment camp was later converted into a hotel. This first hotel on Bonaire was an important step forward for the island. The idea came from the Dutch merchant Lodewijk D. Gerharts, who lived on the island. It was he who suggested to turn the former internment camp, vacant since 1947, into a hotel. At the time the renovation cost well over twenty thousand Antillean guilders, and in 1952 it opened, carrying the beautiful name Hotel Zeebad. A few years later this name was changed to Flamingo Beach Club Hotel. The renovated wooden shacks from the Second World War rendered excellent service until 1973. In that year they were pulled down and at the same site splendid stone bungalows emerged.

Autonomy
On Aruba and Curaçao the rise of the oil industry involved drastic changes. Prosperity as well as political awareness of the Antilleans increased. In 1936 a new Constitution was introduced, which gave all male inhabitants having Dutch nationality the right to vote. The first elections took place in 1937. Political parties, until then completely unknown on the islands, came into being. On Curaçao various political parties were founded, including the Curaçao Roman Catholic Party (1936) and the Democratic Party (1944). The latter party strongly advocated political independence. In the new elections in 1945 this party obtained a very comfortable majority. So the people as well felt that more independence and self-rule were needed. In the meantime the Second World War was coming to an end. As a result of the war, the islands could take their own decisions in various fields. Immediately after the war the issue of self-rule came up again and partly due to the large election victory of the new Democratic Party, a so-called Autonomy Commission left Curaçao for the Netherlands. This commission put up a petition to Queen Wilhelmina, requesting to extend the democratic rights of the Dutch citizens to the Overseas Territories. The petition was fully granted after a parliamentary commission had investigated the situation on the spot in 1947. Shortly afterwards, in 1948, the Curaçao Constitution of 1936 was altered. Another important change took place in 1948 as well, when the Dutch Constitution was reviewed and the term 'Curaçao and dependencies' was replaced by 'Netherlands Antilles'. In the same year the Nationale Volkspartij' was founded on Curaçao. Co-founder Moises Frumencio da Costa Gomez (in Punda, Willemstad there is a

Monument built in 1934 to commemorate 300 jears of Dutch rule

statue dedicated to him in the square bearing his name) played an important part in the realization of the Constitution, in which the autonomy of the island is laid down.

Independence
In the Netherlands people had come to realize that it would be wise to give more autonomy to the last colonies, and on 15 December 1954 Queen Juliana signed the aforementioned treaty, which granted practically complete self-rule to Surinam and the Netherlands Antilles. Autonomy has always been an important political issue on the Netherlands Antilles. The initial to it was given in the time when, because of the oil, the islands (Aruba and Curaçao) prospered. In the 1950s, on the other hand, the oil refining process was increasingly automated. More and more people were dismissed and, also because there were no other sources of income, the number of unemployed grew to unprecedented heights. Since the end of the sixties and the beginning of the seventies, tourism has formed an important source of income and by means of new projects and extensive advertising campaigns one tries to interest vacationists (mainly Americans) in visiting the island.

Tourism
For Bonaire, which has played hardly any part in the whole

process towards self-rule, this new situation meant one could claim technical and financial help on the basis of the Constitution. Therefore, various projects were supported financially by the Netherlands. Industries were developed, including the salt industry, and in the beginning of the 1960s tourism was stimulated. A second hotel, the Bonaire Beach Hotel, was built with the help of development money. This hotel is situated on the Playa de Lechi ('milk beach', the sand is as white as milk there!). In 1962 the hotel was completed and other (private) hotels followed. In 1972 the runway of Flamingo airport, constructed in 1955, was extended to 8,100 feet, to enable larger planes to land there. The increasing tourism gives a boost to the poor economy of the island. Especially the growing dive tourism is of major importance. At the moment everything is being done to make the island as attractive as possible to the dive tourist - without doing harm to the natural beauty the island has both above and under water. If one proceeds carefully in this respect, Bonaire can feel secure about its future. One will have to take care, however, not to destroy the small-scale, intimate character the island now has. At present Bonaire is still an island of calm, and by keeping the hotel capacity limited, its unique character will not be lost.

Beautiful saltpans in Washington-Slagbaai National Park

CHAPTER 3

MAJOR SIGHTS

Bonaire has much more to offer its visitors than just the sun, the sea and the beach. There are a great many things definitely worth visiting. Of course first of all the splendid scenery - above but especially also under water - which you can enjoy in the Washington-Slagbaai National Park and the Bonaire Marine Park. Furthermore, the island has a characteristic architecture with some beautiful country houses in pastel colors as well as small cunucu cottages, caves with mysterious Indian rock drawings, slave huts, centuries-old villages, etc. If you want to have a look at all of this - and I can much recommend that you do - you can book an organised tour at one of the tour operators (see chapter 7 Excursions) or set out by (rented) car yourself. Another possibility - slightly more expensive, but which will take you to all the places you want to visit - is seeing the island by taxi. Taxi drivers are often good guides. If you choose one of the latter possibilities, the following survey of the major sights will be an attractive guideline. Basically Bonaire has two touristic routes: a northern route and a southern route. Both routes start in Kralendijk and lead you along all important sights. The northern route leads you for a great part first along the west coast and then, among other things, to the marina, the studios of Radio Netherlands World Broadcasting, the various hotels and apartment complexes, the water and electricity supply, the transmitting masts of the Radio Netherlands World Broadcasting, Boca di Diabel, country house Karpata, Goto Lake, Washington-Slagbaai National Park, Para Mira, Rincón, Boca Onima and Fontein with Indian rock drawings, Seroe Largo, North Saliña, Antriol and back to Kralendijk. If you take the other touristic route, on the island known as the route 'around the south', then you will pass the village Terra Corá, Flamingo Airport, the Trans World Radio Foundation, a number of apartment complexes, the saltpans of the Antilles International Salt Company, various obelisks and slave huts, Salt Lake, the Flamingo breeding place, the Willemstoren with nearby the stranded vessel Tilisa del Mar, the naturist hotel Sorobon, the lagoon Lac with the peninsula Cai, and by way of the

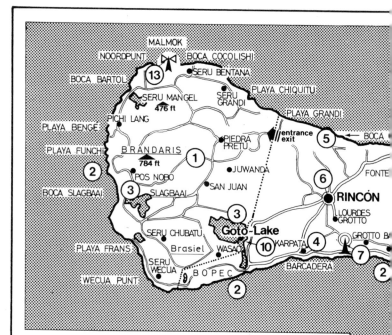

1. Washington-Slagbaai National Park
2. Bonaire Marine Park
3. Flamingos
4. Karpata
5. Indian inscriptions
6. Oldest village Rincón
7. Radio Ned. Wereldomroep Antennae Park
8. Playa Lechi
9. Trans World Radio Studios
10. Observation point
11. Radio Ned. Wereldomroep .udios
12. Klein Bonaire
13. Lighthouse
14. Solar salt works
15. Slave huts / Obelisks
16. Trans World Radio Antennae Park
17. Mangroves
18. Conch shells
19. Lac
20. Rough coast
21. Capital Kralendijk

BONAIRE Sights

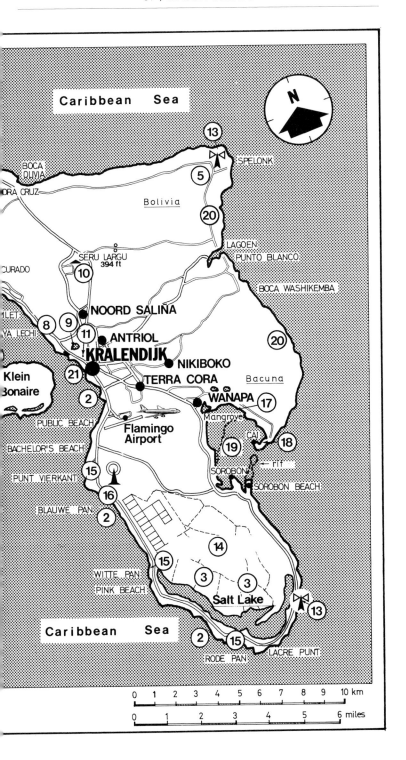

The beautifully restored Passanggrahan

villages Terra Corá and Nikiboko we come back in Kralendijk again. The greater part of the above-mentioned sights
is described in greater detail below. The sights marked with
an asterisk belong to the category 'absolutely not to be
missed'!.

ARCHITECTURE

From the period prior to the discovery, also called Preco-
lumbian (the period before the explorer Christopher Columbus) no buildings have remained. The major architectonic
sights on Bonaire nearly all date back to the Dutch colonial
period of after 1830. The colonists were not allowed to settle on the island, so there are only few buildings that were
constructed earlier. Despite the ban more and more colonists arrived in 1830, and after the lifting of the ban in 1868
the number of colonists increased and accordingly also the
number of buildings. An important part in the realization of,
among other things, public buildings, defensive works and
houses was played by cultural influences, especially from
the Netherlands, the economic possibilities of the island, the
available building material and, last but not least, the climate. All these factors have contributed to the creation of a
Bonairean architecture with a character all its own. Gener-

Dividivi tree with an old country house in the background

ally speaking, the buildings are simple. They usually consist of one story and a roof, are made of local natural stone and subsequently plastered and painted yellow. Some beautiful public buildings in Kralendijk are the modest Fort Oranje, the Administrator's House, dating from 1837 and restored in 1972 and now serving as the Island Office (one of the few buildings from that time consisting of two floors), the Protestant Church from 1847, the former Passanggrahan, restored in 1980 and now used as governmental department and the Island Office dating from 1925. When constructing these buildings, people fell back on to European architectural traditions; however, the climatic circumstances required a special kind of building. All this resulted in a strikingly typical architectural style. This mainly concerned the official residences for the colonists, the public buildings and the country houses. Bonaire has a number of country houses (including Karpata, Santa Barbara, Washikemba, Boven Bolivia, Jatu Bacu), some of which are in good shape again thanks to renovations. The country houses on Bonaire do not have the style of those on Curaçao. In fact, they are hardly more than enlarged houses with an entrance-staircase on the long side. Striking architectural features of the exterior are a tiled roof and (sometimes) a small veranda. In the beginning, bricks were still imported from the Netherlands, but later one started using corallite that was

afterwards plastered with mortar. Since it was not necessary to heat the houses, there were no corridors and the
rooms were all inter-connecting. In order to improve venti-
lation, the country houses often have an oblong floor plan,
with windward bedrooms and a leeward kitchen on the other side. In this way the bedrooms get a lot of cool and fresh
air, and cooking smells cannot penetrate into the house.
Between the bedrooms and the kitchen, there is one long
room or two smaller rooms next to each other. The veranda
on the long side (and sometimes encircling the house) is often covered to offer protection from the sun. For the same
reason the country houses have high saddle roofs with
Dutch tiles, with the attic serving as a buffer against the
heat. The sun can never hit the slanting roof at a right angle. High facades, with or without ornaments, close off the
long roof on the short sides. Furthermore, the slanting roof
has the advantage that the rain is not left on it to evapo-
rate, but is drained away through gutters to special rain
reservoirs. Only colonists could get this kind of house. The
local population and slaves (and afterwards the freed
slaves) lived in simple, self-made huts. These huts, made of
branches and mud and with a hip roof of straw, are called
Cas di Bara in Papiamentu. Until a few years ago some fine
examples could still be seen on Bonaire, but unfortunately
they were all pulled down. The stone version, called Cas di
Piedra, can still be seen in some places, for instance in
Rincón. These dwellings are mostly falling into ruins. The
construction of these houses is very much similar to that of
the huts of the inhabitants of West Africa. It is not sure
whether the slaves took this form of building with them from
Africa, or whether they were confronted with a local Indian
form of building that was hardly different. It is a fact, however, that on the north-west coast of South America this
particular building construction was also used by the local
Indian population, even before the arrival of the African
slaves. These simple houses on Bonaire usually had only
two rooms: one for the parents and one for the children.
Cooking was done outside under a shelter. Later the houses became larger, with more rooms. This type of house is
also called Cunucu-house (Cunucu means countryside). For
some time now there has been a Historic Buildings and An-
cient Monuments Act, and some buildings of cultural-
historical value have now been restored. The country
house Karpata is as magnificent as it used to be in the past,
and some residential houses and governmental buildings
have been renovated. There are also plans to renovate the
old houses at Slagbaai; unfortunately, however, still too

many buildings of historic value are unnecessarily lost. A more active policy in this field is urgently needed.

BOCA SLAGBAAI

The name Slagbaai stands for two things on Bonaire. In the first place it is the name of a plantation (see further Washington-Slagbaai National Park), and secondly a bay - Boca Slagbaai - on the west coast of the island. The name Slagbaai is a corruption of 'Slachtbaai' (Slaughter Bay). In former times this bay was an important natural harbor, from which the salted meat of slaughtered goats was shipped to Curaçao. After 1868 salt as well was exported from here. Some of the buildings are still standing. The largest building served as a salt depot ('magasina'). On the north side of the bay there is an office building (meanwhile restored), where goods were checked in connection with duties on exports. The buildings all date from after 1868 and besides depots and a slaughterhouse, there is a supervisor's house. It is the intention to restore the buildings, which are in poor shape, and to turn them into a tourist attraction (for further information see chapter 2 History).

BONAIRE MARINE PARK

One of the greatest riches of Bonaire is found under water. The magnificent atolls, close under the shore of this island, are among the most beautiful of the world and it is not surprising that during the past ten years the island has developed into one of the most popular diving destinations. Experts consider Bonaire to be one of the three best diving places in the world. As an enthusiast scuba diver I can only confirm this. The underwater world around Bonaire has the beauty of a fairy tale. The atolls are in optimal condition and the fish stock is unique. For that matter, the underwater world of Bonaire is not just of interest to divers, snorkelers too can enjoy all this beauty. Apart from a great many extremely fine diving places (see chapter 6 Major Diving Places), there are many splendid snorkel places to be found. The Caribbean is crystal-clear and often you can look down to a depth of more than 70 feet. Ten years ago there was only one dive center on Bonaire; nowadays there are as many as eight dive centers and their number will no doubt still increase. In spite of the growing diving tourism, the quality of the diving water remains surprisingly good. This is due to the fact that the Bonairean authorities have realized in time that, if no measures were taken, the atolls around the island would not last long. Already in 1971, for instance, a ban on spear fishing was introduced with the result that one can see many big fish, and that the fish are not shy. On the contrary, one dives among the most beautiful fish and some of them (Yellow Snappers, for instance) can even be fed without any trouble. In 1975 a law followed which forbade the gathering and selling of coral (many aquaria lovers took along large pieces of coral and some coral sorts - Black coral was very popular - were used for jewellery). In 1979 a further step was taken and the entire coast of Bonaire was made a protected area and since then the waters around Bonaire, to a depth of 200 feet, have belonged to the underwater park Bonaire Marine Park. A great deal of measures have been taken to protect the fish stock and the coral reefs. Besides the ban on spear fishing and taking coral, a number of new park rules was introduced, such as the ban on damaging coral (by sitting or standing on it) and fishing with other implements than a fishing rod or handline. Furthermore, one is not allowed to anchor in the coral (special anchor buoys have been installed), objects stuck in the coral may not be disengaged, in certain reserves diving or snorkeling is not allowed, etc. All these bans have not been introduced to limit the visitor's freedom, but to keep the coral reefs and fish life in optimal condition so that people will be able to enjoy them for years to come. People also see to it, by means of scientific research, that the increasing use of the reefs does not lead to over-exploitation with all the associated drawbacks. When necessary, for instance, certain (very popular) diving places can be closed temporarily, if necessary even for one or more years, if this is considered to be essential for the mending of the corals.

Thanks to this reef control and observation of the park rules, Bonaire now belongs to the most beautiful diving paradises of the world. The Bonaire Marine Park has been established with financial support of the World Wildlife Fund (for more information about this park, see chapter 1 Flora and Fauna and chapter 6 Major Diving Places).

BRANDARIS

With its 784 feet, the Brandaris is the highest top of Bonaire. The hill is located in the northern part of the island in the Washington-Slagbaai National Park and is made up of rock of volcanic origin: basic lavas, tuff, intrusive bodies,

The Brandaris in Washington-Slagbaai National Park

porphyries and porphyry tuff. The porphyries form magnificent pillar structures here. In the park a walk has been plotted, which leads to top of the Brandaris. Climbing it takes approximately one hour and a half, and for the descent one needs at least one hour. From the top you have a splendid view over the entire island, and in case of extremely clear weather even the Christoffel mountain on Curaçao and the massif of Venezuela can be seen in the distance. (For more information about the Brandaris and its surroundings, see to Washington-Slagbaai National Park.)

CAVES (AND INDIAN ROCK DRAWINGS)

Bonaire has a number of caves that are worth visiting for various reasons. The most important motive, however, is that some caves have beautiful rock drawings, dating from

The caves near Onimá / The Indian rock-drawings near Onimá

the period before the Spanish discovery, and made by the original Indian people. On roughly ten places on Bonaire Indian rock drawings can be seen. The most interesting caves, as far as these Indian rock drawings are concerned, are Onimá, Spelonk and Cueba di Roshikiri. Onimá in fact is not a cave, but a shelter with numerous rock drawings on the underside of a protruding mass of rocks. This spot is found on the grounds of the former plantation of the same name. The way to it is indicated with signs and easy to find. The caves of Spelonk are a bit harder to find.

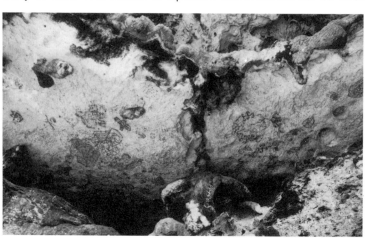

These two caves are on the north coast of Bonaire at about half a mile from the sea. They are spacious caves, the largest is 300 feet deep and on average 66 feet wide and 13 feet high, with numerous stalagmitic columns and a fairly flat floor. On the ceiling of both caves you find a great number of beautiful Indian rock drawings. Also in Cueba di Roshikiri, located half a mile west of Spelonk, rock drawings are found at the nearly 66 feet wide entrance. This cave is about 165 feet deep, 100 feet wide and only 7 feet high. For that matter, the Indian drawings have no recognizable form and until today no one has found out with what purpose they were made. It is presumed religion had to do with it, but that is not sure. Other caves that may be worth visiting but that have no or hardly any Indian rock drawings, are Cueba di Seru Grandi (situated on the grounds of the Washington-Slagbaai National Park), Cueba di Barcadera (situated on plantation Colombia), Cueba di Watapana (near Pos di Watapana), Pos Calbas (Lima), Caranja Grandi (north-east of Punt Vierkant) and Pos Caranja (east of Caranja Grandi).

FLAMINGOS

Bonaire is famous for its orange-red Caribbean flamingos (Phoenicopterus ruber ruber). This flamingo is called Chogogo in Papiamentu (because of the sound it makes). On various spots you can see this majestic bird. This is unique, for in the past centuries the number of nesting places in the Caribbean area has decreased from a good 30 to only four. The progress of civilization is gradually forcing back the Caribbean flamingo. Yet the local authorities are anxious to preserve Bonaire as a suitable breeding ground for this magnificent bird. Especially the quality of the nesting place is of vital importance. The Chogogo is very demanding as far as its breeding place is concerned. The soil must neither be too hard nor too soft, so they can easily build their cone-shaped nests there. The water level must not vary too much, so the nests will not be flooded. Furthermore, the presence of food with a high degree of salt (brine organism) is of great importance, as well as the presence of drinking-water that is not more salty than sea water. And the final important factor is quiet. Absolute quiet! One of the few areas in the world that meets these demands is the Salt Lake on Bonaire. For this reason, too, the flamingo nesting ground is closed for tourists. Without special guidance and permission it is not possible to enter the nesting ground. However, the

The beautiful Goto Lake in the north

flamingos can be observed from a great distance, and out-side of the breeding area they are frequently busy looking for food. In the period 1963-1966 the breeding colony was threatened when the Salt Lake was given in concession to the Antilles Salt Company to start the salt exploitation again. The plans for this area initially threatened the breeding col-ony. However, a solution was reached with stinapa, and an area of 137.5 acres was allotted as a flamingo reserve. This means that the Caribbean flamingo is insured of optimal breeding conditions. Furthermore, the presence of various food areas in the surroundings (apart from the Salt Lake also the Goto Lake and some areas in Venezuela are impor-tant places where food is found) is of great importance. The quality of these areas must be kept in shape, so that this bird, which is so characteristic of Bonaire, will be pre-served.

The beautiful diving place Twixt

Banded butterfly fish

French angel fish

Queen angel fish

Golden tail moray

Green parrot fish

FONTEIN

Plantation in the north-west of Bonaire. The name has been derived from the fact that on the grounds of this plantation there was a fresh water spring. This source is fed from the limestone plateau of Montaña. The stone reservoirs collecting the water were built around 1930 by the plantation owner. However, this plantation decreased in significance and the reservoirs have not been maintained during the last years. At the back is the entrance to a cave where the (fresh) water can be seen to fall down.

GOTO LAKE

Magnificent large salt water lake in the north-west of Bonaire, near the Washington-Slagbaai National Park, separated from the sea by a natural dam (caused by coral forming). The large Goto Lake is one of the spots where the beautiful flamingos can be seen from a short distance. On a high spot there is a number of benches from where you have a good view of this imposing lake, rich in natural beauty, with small isles and magnificent fauna.

KARPATA

Beautifully restored former country house, consisting of a large central part, with on either side a pavilion and furthermore a great many outbuildings. This country house, restored by architect F. Julian, now houses the Ecological Center of the stinapa. Here various natural-scientific researches are carried out. In former times there was also a small fort here to protect the sea connection with Slagbaai against attacks. On the bottom of the sea in front there still lies a gun which belonged to this fort. Presently, next to it a small aloe oven can still be seen, which was in operation until the beginning of the 1950s.

KLEIN BONAIRE

West of Bonaire, at about half a mile off the coast near Kralendijk, there is a small coral isle, appropriately called Klein Bonaire. This uninhabited isle has a surface of about 1,500 acres. It is bare with an occasional low shrub. Klein Bo-

Restored aloe oven at the country house Karpata

naire is especially popular because of its fine dive sites (see chapter 6 Major Dive Sites) which can be found all around the isle. Furthermore regattas are held around the isle and picnic trips are organized as well. Ask at the reception desk of your hotel/apartment if this is possible. From this isle you have a nice view of the west coast of Bonaire.

LAC BAY

North-east of the saltpans on the east coast of Bonaire is a very lovely lagoon, called Lac Bay. In the south-east this inland water is partly separated from the sea by coral reefs just reaching the surface of the water. North of the coral dam, near the tongue of land at Cai, is a canal to the open sea. The inland water is about 3 square miles and very rich in natural beauty. The lagoon has an average depth of about 3 feet and consists of a large open bowl, with on the north side a dense mangrove vegetation and on the south side a wide sandy beach. Here you find the Sorobon Beach

Heaps of Karkó shells near Lac

Hotel, the only naturist hotel of Bonaire (and the whole Caribbean!). The inland lake is especially known for the Karkó, living on the bottom of the lake. The Karkó (Strombus Gigas) is a snail of about one foot long. Its extremities consist of muscles, but the inside is meat which tastes somewhat like chicken, and is therefore edible. Fishermen catch the snails and extract the animal from its shell by making a hole in it. This cancels the vacuum and the snail can simply be taken out. This is the quickest way. So as not to damage the beautifully formed shell, which often has a lovely pink-reddish inside and is a popular souvenir, people proceed as follows: the shell is, for instance, hung on a branch, and a stone is then tied to the snail. After about three hours the snail gives in out of fatigue and lets go of the shell. Not exactly a gentle method. Near Cai, the extreme point of the northern peninsula at Lac, thousands of empty shells (with holes in them!) are piled up. It must be observed that nowadays only small Karkós are caught. The really large beautiful shells that used to be caught, have almost disappeared as a consequence of the excessive catching of snails. Lac Bay is an ideal place of residence for a great number of water birds. Various types of herons can be found, for instance, as well as ospreys, pelicans, terns, frigate-birds and occasionally flamingos. It is also an excellent spawning-bed for a large number of fish, including barracuda (Sphyraena

Mounds consisting of Karkó shells near Lac

barracuda) and snappers (Lutjanidae). In short, Lac Bay is a beautiful wildlife area, certainly worth a visit to those who can appreciate it.

MARCULTURA

Near Captain Don's Habitat is Marcultura, Aquaculture Foundation. Scientific fishing research takes place here: one tries to establish if it is possible to start hatching certain kinds of fish on the ABC-islands, without taking too great financial risks. At the moment the hatching-possibilities of the Karkó(Strombus gigas) are studied, as well as those of various types of shrimps and other fish. Tourists may have a look around here after making an appointment by telephone. The address is: Marcultura, Kaya Gov. Debrot 107, Bonaire, tel. 8595. By the end of 1988 Marcultura will move to a site near Sorobon.

OBELISKS

In the south of Bonaire near the Salt Lake, the former salt-pans, there is still a large number of slave huts with some obelisk or pyramid shaped stone buildings. These historic buildings had a practical, not a religious function. At the beginning of the nineteenth century the exploitation of the saltpans was very remunerative. In 1837 four colored obelisks were erected near the saltpans in the south, so that the ships coming to pick up the salt would have a proper landmark. The obelisks were painted red, white, blue and orange (the colors of the Dutch flag and the Royal House). At the most southern saltpans - called Red Pan - was a tall flagpole, on which a red, white, blue or orange flag was hoisted to point out to the ships where they had to be: at Red Pan, Blue Pan, White Pan or Orange Pan. The colored obelisks were clearly to be seen from sea and the ships could come to anchor close to the obelisks. Three of the four obelisks are still to be seen, the orange obelisk was destroyed. The obelisks that are still intact give the landscape in the south a character all its own.

PARA MIRA

Literally this means 'observation-post' in Papiamentu and that is exactly what it is. At Para Mira one has a splendid

Obelisk with slave huts on the left

view of the oldest village of the island, Rincón. It is certainly worth-while to make some pictures of the nice view from here.

Radio Netherlands World Broadcasting

RADIO NETHERLANDS MUSEUM & WORLD BROADCASTING COMPANY

On 15 April 1947 Radio Netherlands World Broadcasting was founded with the purpose of informing, by means of daily broadcasts, Dutch, Antillean and Surinam people abroad and in the Overseas Territories of what was going on in the Netherlands. Special broadcasts are produced for the Netherlands Antilles. In 1969 two short-wave transmitters were installed on Bonaire, in order to receive the radio signals from the Netherlands and then to amplify and transmit them. So no programs are made here; they are merely received, amplified and then broadcast again. In a small museum in the building, old transmitting equipment can be admired.

SALT LAKE

In former days this oblong, narrow salt lake in the south of Bonaire was separated from the sea by a small dam of coral rock. Nowadays it has an open connection with the sea, for the purpose of the current salt production by the Antilles International Salt Company. Because of this, the salt level has decreased. As a result, the flamingos moved to a saltier area in the north, where the salt extraction now takes place. The Salt Lake still has a purple glow due to the relatively high salt level, which underthe bright sun provides a surrealistic spectacle. Along the Salt Lake one finds the famous slave huts with the colored obelisks.

SALTPANS AND SALT PRODUCTION

Salt has played an important part in the history of Bonaire (see chapter 2 History). The presence of this natural preservative made the island interesting in the eyes of many. At the end of the sixteenth and the beginning of the seventeenth century herring-fishing was an important livelihood for the Dutch. The herring were salted and could thus be preserved. Without salt they would have rotted within a few days. So salt was of vital importance for herring-fishing and the trade involved. Initially, one obtained the salt from Spain and Portugal, but when at the time of the Eighty Years' War between the Netherlands and Spain the Dutch could no longer obtain their salt on the Iberian peninsula, they had to find new saltpans. These were found in South America (Venezuela) and later in the Caribbean, especially on St Maarten. This island was conquered, but was lost again in 1633 and the Dutch were forced to find other saltpans. It

Glistening salt heaps

was decided to take Curaçao, and when this island had been captured from the Spaniards in 1634, a salt expert was sent to adjoining Bonaire to establish whether the salt-pans there were of good quality. They were, and soon the Dutch started to exploit them. Much manpower was need-ed, and for this purpose black slaves were brought to the island to produce the salt. In nature salt (NaCl) is found dis-solved in water, and in a solid form. The salt seawater evaporated in the saltpans close to the sea (the Salt Lake, for instance). After evaporation of the water, salt remains. This process can be witnessed at the many saltpans (Saliñas, in Papiamentu) Bonaire still has. Because of the evaporation the water becomes increasingly saltier, and it gets a violet glow in the bright sun. After evaporation of all the water, the slaves scooped the raw sea salt out of the pans, after which it was to dry in big heaps. Subsequently, it was shipped to the Netherlands. In the long run, however, this did not pay, and especially when after the emancipation of the slaves one had to start hiring workers, the exploita-tion of the saltpans came to an end. It was not until 1966 that the salt production on Bonaire was taken up again. Two years earlier, the old saltpans near the Salt Lake were conceded to the Antilles International Salt Company, a sub-sidiary of the International Salt Company from the United States, and in 1966 the exploitation was started. In 1967 the saltpans and the plant were extended and modernized. Nowadays the salt is still being made by means of the natu-ral process of evaporation. It is lent a hand, however. Via a special dam the sea water is pumped into special condens-ers, and under the influence of the sun the crystallization process starts. After some time the water is pumped into special crystallization basins and after approximately a year the salt can be extracted. It is then sieved, washed and stored in heaps. Finally, a modern conveyor-belt carries it to the shipping pier from where it is transported by ship. The export of salt has in the meantime developed once more into a substantial pillar of the Bonairean economy.

SLAVE HUTS

On the dam, separating the Salt Lake from the sea, there are on two places, where the slaves used to make salt, some tens of slave huts. On weekdays these stone huts served as shelters for the slaves, who on Monday came walking to these saltpans from Rincón and later from Antriol. They stayed the whole week, to walk back again to their

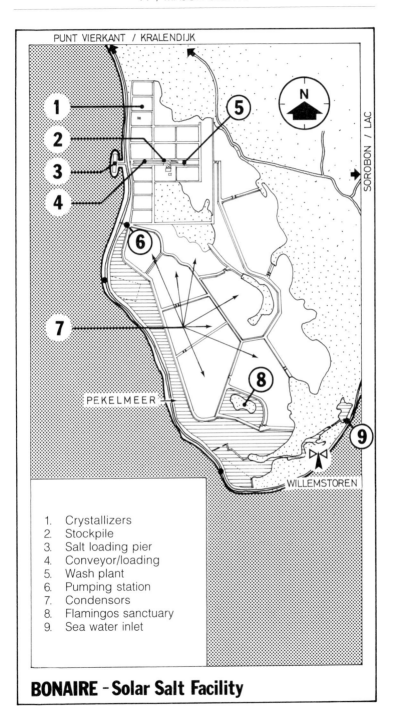

PUNT VIERKANT / KRALENDIJK

N

SOROBON / LAC

PEKELMEER

WILLEMSTOREN

1. Crystallizers
2. Stockpile
3. Salt loading pier
4. Conveyor/loading
5. Wash plant
6. Pumping station
7. Condensors
8. Flamingos sanctuary
9. Sea water inlet

BONAIRE - Solar Salt Facility

The small slave huts near the Salt Lake

homes on Saturday. The walk from Rincón to the saltpans took about seven hours. At night the slaves slept two by two in simple mud huts with roofs made of leaves. By the middle of the nineteenth century these simple mud huts were replaced by slave houses made of stone. These huts had gone to ruin, but with financial support from the Netherlands they have been restored by the stinapa. If you take a look at them, it will be obvious that the small stone huts - the roof reaches as far as the waist - cannot really be called comfortable. Nowadays tourists sometimes spend the night there.

TRANSWORLD RADIO STUDIOS

On 11 February 1952 Trans World Radio was founded in Greensboro, United States. A Protestant society with the aim of spreading the gospel by means of radio broadcasts. In 1962 a studio and a vast transmitting station were built on Bonaire, and on 13 August 1964 the first broadcast took place. Nowadays, there are weekly programs from Bonaire in more than 15 languages, which are broadcast all over the world. The foundation has another transmitter in Monte Carlo and several studios around the world.

Restored cottage in Washington-Slagbaai National Park

WASHINGTON-SLAGBAAI NATIONAL PARK

In the north-west of the island is a large national park of a good 13,500 acres, called Washington-Slagbaaai National Park. This lovely park is one of the most beautiful spots of the Antilles. It covers the entire north-west of the island, and was opened on 8 May 1969, being the first national park on all of the Netherlands Antilles (meanwhile there are more). It is run by the Netherlands Antilles National Park Foundation (in Dutch: Stichting Nationale Parken Nederland-

The entrance of Washington-Slagbaai National Park

se Antillen, in short stinapa). This foundation was established in 1962 with the aim of acquiring, preserving and
protecting those areas of land and water that are of great
importance because of natural and scenic beauty, or because the indigenous flora and fauna are threatened. Objects of geological, archaeological or historical value are
also included. The next objective is to open these areas to
the public - population as well as tourists - for recreational
and educational purposes. In this way one hopes to protect
the vulnerable countryside, threatened more and more,
from the consequences of the strong population growth
and the increasing tourism. In 1968 the national government bought the Washington plantation and turned the
management over to the stinapa. This initiated the Washington-Slagbaai National Park. The genesis of the park even
goes back to the last century. From the beginning of the colonial Dutch period in 1636 (see chapter 2 History) Bonaire
had been government-owned: the island was one large
government plantation. After the so-called Emancipation-
Regulation had been issued in 1862, putting an end to slavery, all slaves on the islands were released. This also ended
the successful exploitation of the island, because it turned
out to be too expensive to continue the various plantations
with hired workers. The colonial authorities were forced to
sell the land. In 1868 the whole north-western part of the
island was sold in two lots. The southern lot, called Brasiel,
was sold for Hfl. 22,000.- to private individuals and the
northern lot, Slagbaai, was disposed of for Hfl. 35,200.-.
The lots became the property of Moises Jacob Jesurun,
John Frederik Neuman, August Wilhelm Neuman and Cas-

per Lodewijk Neuman. In 1892 the lands changed hands: Jean Luis Joaquin Cadieres and Jean Jacques Debrot bought the plantation Slagbaai for the sum of Hfl. 33,250.-. In 1920 the northern part of the plantation was sold to the brothers Julio Eustaquio Rosa Herrera and Gijsberto Rafael Eduvigis Herrera for the sum of Hfl. 45,000.-. They called their plantation America and went ahead energetically. They built a new entrance, as well as a number of offices and depots. Here the laborers were paid and soon this place was called Washington. Why? Because it was the most important spot of the plantation and the capital of America is called Washington. Gradually this name established itself and soon the plantation was popularly called Washington (by the laborers). In 1931 Julio Herrera died, which put an end to the cooperation of the two brothers. In 1940 the plantation passed into the hands of the eldest son, Julio Caesar (Boy) Herrera, who had been in charge of the plantation since 1936. During the years that followed, he turned the plantation into a successful enterprise. In 1967 Boy Herrera fell ill, and because he feared his heirs might sell the plantation to foreign speculators, who would be likely to ruin his beautiful plantation in order to built larger hotels, before his death he arranged the sale of his plantation. He offered the whole of it for a moderate price to the gov-

Wind-determined dividivi

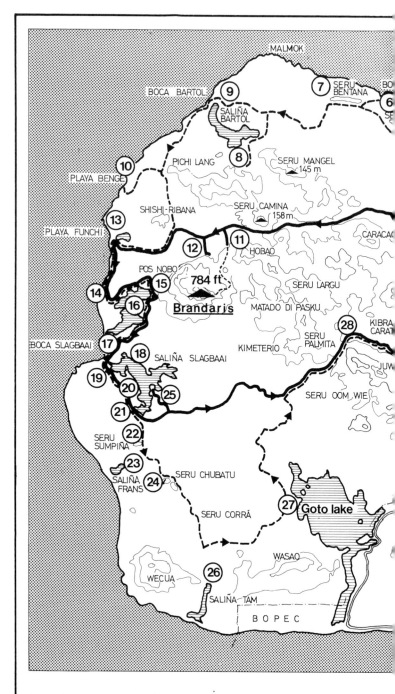

Washington ~ Slagbaai   NATIONAL PARK

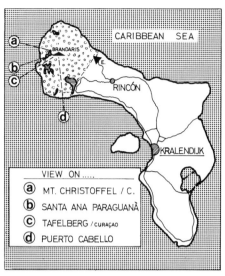

VIEW ON .....

ⓐ MT. CHRISTOFFEL / C.
ⓑ SANTA ANA PARAGUANÀ
ⓒ TAFELBERG / CURAÇAO
ⓓ PUERTO CABELLO

WASHINGTON-SLAGBAAI
NATIONAL PARK

1.   Entrance/exit
2.   Saliña Matthijs
3.   Playa Chiquitu
4.   Boca Chiquitu
5.   Seru Grandi
6.   Boca Cocolishi
7.   Seru Bentana
8.   Pos'i Mangel
9.   Boca Bartol
10. Playa Bengé
11. Subi Brandaris
12. Put Bronswinkel
13. Playa Funchi
14. Wajacá
15. Pos Nobo
16. Saliña Wajacá
17. Boca Slagbaai
18. Saliña Slagbaai
19. Aloë-'kitchen'
20. Panorama Slagbaai
21. Cactusdeformations
22. Seru Sumpiña
23. Saliña Frans
24. Seru Chubatu
25. Flamingo observation
26. Saliña Tam
27. Goto Lake / flamingo observation
28. Juwa Pas

ernment, provided they would guarantee the plantation would remain in its current state and that no hotels or motels or the like would be built there. It was his most fervent wish that it would be a nature reserve. A wish that has come true. On 16 November 1967 Boy Herrera died, and on 7 December 1968 the Washington plantation was bought with financial support from the Netherlands. The very same day the management of this beautiful area was turned over to the stinapa. On 9 May 1969 it was officially opened by the son of one of the former owners of the plantation, His Excellency Nicolaas Debrot, Governor of the Netherlands Antilles. The first national park was a fact: over 880 acres of beautiful scenery with a great variety of landscapes, from splendid bays with an azure-blue sea (with magnificent coral reefs below the surface), via large plains with flowering bulb cacti and towering candle cacti to beautifully ranges of hills. The Washington-Slagbaai National Park attracted an ever increasing number of visitors from home and abroad. In 1977 a long-standing wish was fulfilled: after years of vain attempts, the stinapa succeeded in buying the adjoining plantation Slagbaai. Already in 1966 attempts had been made to obtain this plantation, but its owner, J.H.R. Beaujon initially did not want to sell it. However, in 1971 he informed the stinapa that under certain conditions he was willing to sell. His wish was that his territory too would be used exclusively as a national park, a wish readily granted by the stinapa. Nevertheless, it was only after his death on 17 July 1976, that the stinapa could conclude the transaction. The heirs respected Beaujon's wish, and on 23 September 1977 the stinapa bought the plantation Slagbaai for the sum of Hfl. 1,500,000.-. This amount was raised with the help of subsidies and gifts. After having been separated for nearly 60 years, the Washington and Slagbaai plantations were re-united. After a request from the stinapa to the national government, the foundation was given supervision over the remaining part of north-west Bonaire, Brasiel plantation in the south-west, and nearby Goto Lake. A small part of Brasiel plantation had been conceded to an oil transshipment company. This part, however, is located near the coast and separated from the northern part by a range of hills. It is not a disturbing factor. The total area which the stinapa has managed since then, measures 13,500 acres. A plan was made, and Jan Blok of the Agricultural University of Wageningen (the Netherlands) was enlisted to develop a network of roads for the park. He plotted three routes through the most beautiful parts, and on 12 May 1979 the (renovated) park, now called Washington-Slagbaai National

Junction of the green (short) and yellow (long) route

Park, was officially re-opened by the Governor of Bonaire, mr A.R.W. Sint Jago.

Routes
The park is open every day, except on public holidays, from 8.00 a.m. to 5.00 p.m. Admission is Naƒ 3.50 ($ 2.-) per person, and children under fifteen only pay Naƒ 0.50. It is easy to find: drive towards Rincón, follow the green signposts, and after a few miles the asphalt road becomes an unpaved road, called Kaya Gilberto R.E. Herrera. At the junction take the road to the left (the road to the right goes to Playa Grandi). This road is alternately paved and unpaved and leads you to the entrance of the park, consisting of a few buildings. In the building to the left you can buy an admission ticket. Here there is also an exhibition to be seen about the development of the park. Immediately after entering the park it becomes obvious that this nature reserve is characterized by a much varied landscape: there you can find vast saline plains (saliñas), extended areas with low brush-wood and towering candle cacti, steep hills with beautiful views, magnificent inland bays with beautiful atolls below the surface, aloe fields, etc. Therefore, a tour through the park is certainly no boring event. On the contrary, the scenery changes every few miles, and it is quite an experience as far as flora and fauna are concerned. Three routes have been plotted in the park, a walking tour (or rather: a climbing tour!) and two car routes. There is a short route of about 15 miles (indicated by small green flags)

and a somewhat longer route of about 21 miles (with small yellow flags). At the entrance of the park you can obtain a simple map, showing the various routes. For the amount of Naƒ 7.50 you can also buy a beautiful guide, in English, containing many color pictures, called Excursion-Guide to the Washington-Slagbaai National Park, Bonaire. This guide gives detailed descriptions of the routes, and about 30 spots are elaborately described. These spots are numbered and marked along the route. The short, green route partly overlaps the long, yellow route. For the rest, you should also observe that on these car routes a maximum speed of about 40 miles per hour is reasonable. Not only to disturb the animals as little as possible, but especially to spare the (rented) car and its passengers. For the roads all are un-paved, so one should be careful. Whichever route you choose, the long or the short one, some spots are definitely worth a visit and should not be missed. Below, a survey of the two routes, mentioning in particular the spots you defi-nitely should see.

The yellow route (21 miles)

The long route is indicated by small yellow flags. Immediate-ly after entering the park you pass (at entrance no. 1) some beautiful cactus species, such as the candle cacti Yatu (Le-maireocereus griseus) and Kadushi (Cereus repandus), and the disc cactus Prickley-pear (Opuntia wentiana). Further-more, you can here admire, among other things, the Kuida (Prosopis juliflora), Wild Sage (Croton flavens) and Aloe (Aloe barbadensis). When the Aloe is flowering, you also find many Chibichibis here (on the other Leeward Islands called: Barica Heel) or Bananaquits (Coereba flaveola). This lovely songbird is often very tame and likes to show up near people. The yellow belly is a sign it is a Chibichibi. On Bo-naire this bird is called in full Chibichibi bachi pretu, literally translated meaning 'black coat'. Furthermore, a lot of Blue-tailed Emeralds (Chlorostilbon mellisuqus) and Ruby-Topaz Humming-birds (Chrysolampis mosquitus) are to be found here. These birds are attracted by the nectar and can be recognized by the fast wingbeats, giving the impression they 'stand still' in the air while sucking the nectar from the flowers. A bit further down the road you see to the right Saliña Matthijs (no. 2). When the saltpans are flooded in the rainy season (November), here you can see Flamingos (Phoenicopterus ruber), Dunlins (Calidris), Black-winged Stilts (Himantopus himantopus) and other birds. For the greater part of the year, however, the saltpans are dry (and one can see these birds at other saltpans). Sometimes here you find a Bahama Pintail (Anas bahamensis). Here you can also take a close look at the tree species Oliba (Capparis odoratissima) with its dark green top and the famous wind-shaped Divi-divi (Caesalpina coriaria). The Divi-divi or Watapana is a characteristic tree with double-formed compound leaves. The leaflets have a size of about 1 to 5 mm, and the flowers are a yellowish white and strongly fragrant. Until quite recently for many Bonaireans these trees were a major means of support. Its pod contains tannin, that used to be exported (until 1954). The tannin was used in the manufacturing of leather. Here is also found a specific species of candle cactus with a yellow top and white hairs between the needles (Cephalocereus lanuginosus). Somewhat further on the short and the long route split up: the road to the left is the short route, with green signposts, and to the right is the long route, indicated by yellow signposts. If we follow the yellow route, we eventually end up at the north coast. Here we can visit, among other things, Playa Chiquitu (no. 3), a small idyllic beach where people like to picnic. A warning is called for here: it is wise not to let the water reach higher than your hips; especially, do not go swimming! The currents are perilous here. A bit more to the north we find Boca Chiquitu (no. 4), an inlet in the coast. On the water one often finds floating brown seaweed (Sargassum), and many fossils can be seen in the limestone rocks here. The attentive visitor may also find beautiful shells, including the 'Infant-in-arms' (Cerion uva). Still somewhat more to the north is Seru Grandi (no. 5), a limestone terrace that must have been under water in former times. When we continue our way, we pass Cara Corrá, meaning in Papiamentu 'red face'. This name becomes clear when we see the rockwork here, which resembles the face of an Indian. A bit further we come to Boca Cocolishi (no. 6). This name means 'bay shell', and here you find a great diversity of shells and shells' remains. The many algae in the water lend the water an intriguing purple glow. Following the yellow signposts we pass Ceru Bentana (no. 7). Here is a lighthouse, and from the top of the hill we have a nice view of Sabana. A little further we arrive at the first fresh water well, Pos Mangel (no. 8). This well can supply fresh water throughout the year and is therefore a meeting place of a great many bird species. Leave the car in the parking lot, walk on carefully to the well and sit down quietly. To bird lovers this spot usually is a high light in their visit to the park. The following bird species may be seen here: Bananaquit, Black-faced Grass quit (Tiaris bicolor), Yellow Warbler (Dendroica petechia), Tropical Mocking-Bird (Mimus gilvus),

Common Ground dove, (Columbigallina passerina), White-fronted dove, (Leptotila verreauxi), Eared dove (Zenaida auriculata) and ten species of Fly-catchers (Tyrannidae). If you are lucky, you can also see here the Yellow-winged Parrot or Lora (Amazona barbadensis rothschildi). This rare Amazon parrot can be recognized by its bright green and yellow head, and is only found on Bonaire. Unfortunately the species is threatened with extinction. In former times they were taken out of their nests when they were young and sold on Curaçao for prices varying from Naƒ 40.- to Naƒ 150.- or more, because they are popular cage birds. The reason for this is that the Lora, when young, can rather simply be taught to 'speak'. Since 1952 the Lora has been protected by law, but during a number of extremely dry years (1977, for instance) their number has decreased considerably, and there are still people who catch them in order to sell them. Their number is now estimated at approximately a hundred. They are brooding from May till August, and a nest often contains not more than one or two young. It is to be hoped there will be more supervision and that poachers, if any, will be punished severely, so that the number of Loras will soon increase again. On our way to the

Bocá Slagbaai with the ruins of the old slaughterhouse

next stop, we pass on the left Saliña Bartol. At these salt-pans often flamingos are to be seen in the distance. The next stop on this route is Boca Bartol (no. 9). Here you can find the Snowy Egret (Egretta thula), the Brown Pelican (Pelecanus occidentalis), the Neotropic Cormorant (Phalacrocorax olivaceus) and other birds. With a bit of luck you can also see the Brown Booby (Sula leucogaster) here. This bird catches fish in a spectacular way. By diving down from a great height, its wings pressed against the body, this bird collects its meal. A method applied successfully by the Brown pelican as well. The next stop is Playa Bengé (no. 10), a popular place for picnicking and snorkeling. This spot is one of the finest snorkeling spots of the island. Here the most beautiful fish can be admired. Further on the road goes inland and bends round the hill of Shishiribana. Here the long and the short routes come together, and the road continues in the direction of the coast - along this road we find many Barba di palus (Tillandsia recurvata) - to end at Playa Funchi (no. 13). Again we see some saliñas and flamingos here and by the waterside Ruddy Turnstones (Arenaria interpres) and Black-winged Stilts (Himantopus himantopus) looking for food. Furthermore this bay houses a lot of lizards (Cnemidophorus murinus ruthveni), which are very shy. This type is found only on the island. The only snake species of the island is also to be seen here, the harmless Silversnake (Leptotyphlops albifrons), and also the Yellow Scorpion (Centruroides hasethi). A sting from this scorpion may hurt, but aside from that it is harmless. The chance that you will come across one, is quite small, however, because the animals are very shy. We continue our way along the coast and pass the gate that used to separate Slagbaai plantation from Washington plantation. On this road you come across many iguanas (Iguana iguana). This reptile species is considered to be a delicacy by the Antilleans (it tastes somewhat of chicken) and eating it is said to increase the potency (the iguana has two penises). They are still hunted, and so it is not surprising that the iguanas are shy. Along this coastal road there are many Dyewood trees (Haematoxylon brasiletto) and Palu hukus (Jacquinia barbasco). The Dyewood trees used to be popular because of their saps, which were used for making coloring matters. In the past the sap of the Palu hukus was used by the Indians to catch fish. They threw cracked leaves, branches or berries of this tree into the water, and the fish that ate these were drugged and came floating to the surface. The sap of this tree is poisonous to fish, but harmless to man. This fishing method is still applied by the Indians on the continent of

South America. When the coastal road goes inland again, we pass Wajacá (no. 14), from where we have a nice view of Slagbaai. Land inward is Pos Nobo (no. 15), which is Papiamentu for 'new well'. Here too many birds are found. From here you can climb the Brandaris, but this route is not signposted. A bit further we have a nice view of the salt-pans of Saliña Wajacá (no. 16), after which we arrive at Boca Slagbaai (no. 17). This is an ideal place to stop for swimming or snorkeling. The name Slagbaai is a corruption of 'Slachtbaai' (Slaughter Bay). In former times this was an important harbor, from where the salted meat of slaughtered goats was shipped to Curaçao. After 1868 salt as well was exported from here. The tallest building you see here used to be the depot ('magasina') in which the salt was stored. On the north side of the bay is an office building (meanwhile restored), where goods were checked in connection with duties on exports. The buildings all date from after 1868, and apart from depots and a slaughterhouse, the supervisor's house is still standing. It is the intention to restore the buildings, which are in poor shape, and to turn them into a tourist attraction. The buildings were all built on the natural dam between the sea and the saltpans behind. Also in this Saliña Slagbaai (no. 18) flamingos may be admired. North of the 'Magasina' some calabash trees (Crescentia cujete) grow. The bay is frequently visited by the Reddish Egret (Egretta rufescens), which can be recognized by its white coat. Occasionally you may see, high in the sky, the White-tailed Hawk (Buteo albicaudatus) hunting for lizards and small birds. Continuing our way we pass a great many aloes (Aloe barbadensis), the remains of what once was a large aloe plantation. An aloe oven (no. 19) is the silent witness of what used to be an important source of income for the island. Somewhat further there is again a nice view of Slagbaai (no. 20). Immediately past some very fascinating cactus formations (no. 21) we arrive at the second junction of the yellow and the green route. We keep right and follow the 'panorama road', thus called because it offers beautiful views of Slagbaai, Seru Sumpiña (no. 22), Saliña Frans (no. 23), Ceru Chubatu (no. 24), Saliña Tam (no. 26) and Goto Lake (no. 27). From the top of the hill Seru Sumpiña we have a nice view of Slagbaai and the Brandaris. On the top of the Seru Sumpiña we find, among other things, Passion-flowers (Passiflora foetida). Further on the road goes down steeply, and we see Saliña Frans on the right; then we go up again to Seru Chubatu. Here we see a great many climbing plants (Cynanchum). The next hill has a red color and is therefore called Ceru Corrá, it con-

Put Bronswinkel in Washington-Slagbaai National Park

sists almost entirely of pure quartz, and the red color is caused by the high degree of iron. From the next hill we have a fine panoramic view south toward Saliña Tam and east toward Goto Lake, our next stop. From the Flamingo Observation post (near no. 27) the famous orange-red Caribbean flamingo (Phoenicopterus ruber ruber) can be observed excellently. A pair of binoculars is nevertheless no luxury, for the flamingos are very shy and, if approached, fly away quickly, so it is wise to keep some distance. Especially during the breeding season - from January till July - Goto Lake is an important feeding place for the flamingos which, for that matter, brood only in the saltpans near Orange Pan in the south of Bonaire. The yellow route continues northward across the plain of Slagbaai along aloe fields and large quantities of thorned vegetation, and then joins the short, green route again. Both routes now stay together until the entrance/exit of the park. Along this route we find, among other things, many West-Indian Birches (Bursera simaruba) and Palu di sia blankus (Bursera bonairensis). The West-Indian Birch can be recognized by its red bark. On some spots along this road French Cotton (Calotropis procera) is found, identifiable by the white/violet flowers. The road gradually starts to climb again and here we find much pockwood (Guaiacum officinale). In the flowering time the tree is full of beautiful blue flowers and bears heart-shaped orange fruit. Further on we come to Juwa Pas (no. 28) with beautiful views. To the south west is Ceru Wecua (526 ft), the highest hill of Brasiel, and far away in the south we see Goto Lake. To the north we have a nice view of Washington plantation from here, and in the west we see the hill Ceru Palmita (357.5 ft). From here we also see the 485.5 ft high hill Kibra Carati (no. 29), which is completely covered with Kibrahacha (Tabebuia billbergii). This tree has no leaves, but only flowers and when these are in bloom, the whole hill is covered with yellow flowers. However, this is only the case during a few days per year (mostly in April). Then the road goes down steeply and further on to the left we see various Agave species (Agave vivipara, for instance). To the right of the road is the West Indian Cherry Tree (Malpighia punicifolia). The fruit of this tree is full of vitamin C and very tasty. In this area the Bringamosa (Cnidoscolus urens) also grows, identifiable by its hand-shaped leaves. Do not touch these, for the fine hair on the branches secretes a caustic substance, causing a burning feeling and an irritated skin. If we continue our way and keep to the right, we automatically end up at the park entrance/exit.

The green route
The short route (15 miles long) for a great part overlaps the long, yellow route. Part of this route has already been described above. If you opt for the short route, at the junction you take the road to the left and then follow the green signposts. This road leads you along an abundance of candle cacti (Lemaireocereus griseus) and Prickly-pears (Opuntia wentiana). A bit further, to the right of the road, you can see the wind-shaped Divi-divi or Watapana trees. A little bit further we pass a dried-up river valley, after heavy rains briefly containing some water. Shortly after it has rained, the water speeds down through these valleys. Usually they are completely dry (from February till September). From the hill Seru Kepton we have a nice view of the west coast. To the left is the highest hill of Bonaire, the Brandaris (784 ft). At our next stop Subi Brandaris (no. 11) is the starting point of

the third route, the walking tour taking you to the top of the Brandaris. From the top you have a splendid view of the whole island and in case of extremely clear weather, you can even discern the mountain of Christoffel on Curaçao and the mountains of Venezuela in the distance. The climb up takes about one hour and a half and it takes at least one hour to go down. It is wise to start climbing as early as possible, in view of the quickly rising temperature. Be sure to take plenty of water with you! Those who persevere are rewarded with an extremely beautiful panorama of the island. At the foot of the Brandaris, near the parking lot, the trees bear a great many Barba di palus (Tillandsia recurvata). The next spot of interest is Put Bronswinkel (No. 12). Here again the trees bear many Barba di palus. Just like Pos'i Mangel (no. 8) this well has fresh water throughout the year and it attracts a great variety of birds. Park the car and slowly walk the last part. Birds you can find here are, among others, the Pearly-eyed Thrasher (Margarops fuscatus), the Yellow oriole (Icterus nigrogularis), the Scaly-naped pigeon (Columba squamosa), the Bare-eyed Pigeon (Columba corensis), White-fronted dove (Leptotila verreauxi), the Eared Dove (Zenaida auriculata), the Common ground dove(Columbigallina passerina), the Big Grey Flycatchers (Tyrannus dominicensus), the Small Yellow Flycatchers (Sublegatus modestus), and the Small Grey Flycatchers (Elaenia martinica). Furthermore, you can here see Bananaquits, Tropical Mocking-birds and Yellow Warblers, but they are to be found in great numbers throughout the park. For that matter, there are also a great many midges near this well. If we walk quietly back to the car and continue our way, the green and yellow routes come together again after about half a mile. Both routes split up once more beyond Saliña Slagbaai. The green route keeps to the left. Further on we turn to the left and then arrive at a Flamingo Island (no. 25), again a beautiful observation post for watching the flamingos in Saliña Slagbaai. The road continues across the plain of Slagbaai with on your left the Brandaris, and after a few miles joins the yellow route again (for the remaining part of the route, see no. 28 yellow route).

Nature conservation

From the above it will be clear that a visit to the Washington-Slagbaai National Park is definitely worth-while. Take your time for it and if possible, take the long route (34 km). Do realize there are no restaurants or ice-cream men along the road, so if you intend to spend some time in the park, it

The Willemstoren, the oldst lighthouse on Bonaire

is wise to take along food and especially something to drink. Take care as well you have enough gas in your tank, ánd before entering the park check your tires and the spare tire. Also check if the (rented) car has a jack. Furthermore: observe the park rules! Do not leave the indicated paths, drive in the indicated direction, do not make fire, do not leave litter and do not in any way disturb the peace of the animals. Catching and/or killing animals is strictly forbidden, as is the removing of eggs. Drive carefully and take care when swimming in the bays on the north-east coast. After a visit to this magnificent national park it will be clear what excellent work the stinapa has been doing here during the last few years. It is to be hoped this work will be continued for a long time to come and that this unique area will be kept in its natural state for ever. For more information: stinapa, c/o P.O. Box 2090, Curaçao, Netherlands Antilles.

WILLEMSTOREN

On the most southern point of Bonaire, a little to the east, is the Willemstoren, the oldest lighthouse of Bonaire. This lighthouse was built in 1837 and 1838 and has the shape of a Doric pillar. As early as 1730, people were planning to build a lighthouse here, but the idea was rejected because a lighthouse would also serve as a beacon for enemy ships. But when a number of their own ships had been wrecked, people decided to build a kind of lighthouse here after all and in 1762 a pile of stones, with a fire burning at night, was erected here. In spite of this beacon, still a number of ships ran aground and it was then decided to build a real lighthouse. On 24 August 1838, the birthday of King Willem I, the lamp of the new lighthouse was lit for the first time. The lighthouse was named after the king.Later more lighthouses were built, at Punt Vierkant, Spelonk and Boca Cocolishi. The Willemstoren, however, is the oldest lighthouse of Bonaire.

CITIES

ANTRIOL

Small village north east of Kralendijk. Its name has been derived from the Spanish al interior, which is supposed to refer to the fact that around 1620 some Spaniards settled here - 'inland', hence the name -. Throughout the ages the village, just like Kralendijk and the more northerly North Saliña, has grown and now these places have almost become one. Nowadays Antriol has about 1,700 inhabitants.

Kralendijk seen from the north

The fish market in Roman style

Monument commemorating the landing of Van Walbeeck in 1634

Glistening salt heaps

Salt production near the Pekelmeer

Next page: The Brandaris in the National Park Washington-Slagbaai

Sunset at Playa Lechi

KRALENDIJK

About 1810 Kralendijk came into existence around the natural harbor on this spot. Here the Dutch had built a small
fort, Fort Oranje, in order to protect the island from invaders. The fort, built at the end of the eighteenth century, was
the house of the Commander until 1837. Afterwards it
served for a long time as a depot of government's goods
and it was also a prison for some time. About 1868 a wood-
en lighthouse was built in the fort, which was replaced by a
stone tower in 1932. Nowadays the Harbor Office and the
Public Cleansing Department have their offices in the fort.
The islanders still call Kralendijk, Playa (beach). For a long
time the colonists were not allowed to settle on the island.
In spite of this ban new inhabitants settled here from
abroad, and Playa gradually developed into a small town.
Various houses were built, such as the Governor's house in
1837. This beautiful house was restored in 1973 and now
accommodates the Island Council. Here the Island Government resides. It was only in 1840 that the name of Kralendijk became popular. This name is derived from the place of
settling, which was on a dike of coral rock. Apart from Fort
Oranje and the former Governor's House, other interesting
buildings are to be seen in Kralendijk. Near the harbor, for
instance, is a small fish market, built in 1935 in Roman style.
The center of the town is Wilhelmina Square. Right in the
middle of the square is the small Protestant church, built in
1857. In the park is an obelisk in memory of the 300 years
of Dutch government, starting with the landing of Van Walbeeck on 26 July 1634. This monument was erected in
1934. Opposite is a more modern monument in memory of
the 34 Bonaireans who were killed during the Second
World War. Furthermore, there is a beautifully restored
building in this square housing the seat of the Island Council
and the council hall. Kralendijk has a main street: the wide
Kaya Grandi, running from north to south. Here you can
find the Tourist Board Office, for instance, the General Post
Office, Hotel Rochaline, a number of restaurants and most
of the shops. A walk through Kralendijk is certainly worth
while.

NIKIBOKO

Small village east of Kralendijk, with approximately 900 inhabitants. Has gradually developed into an outskirt of Kra-

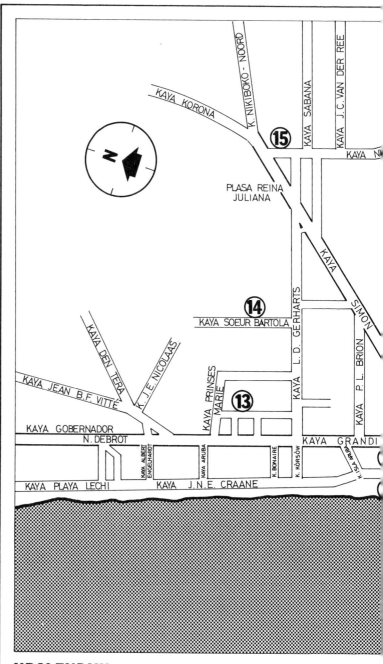

KRALENDIJK

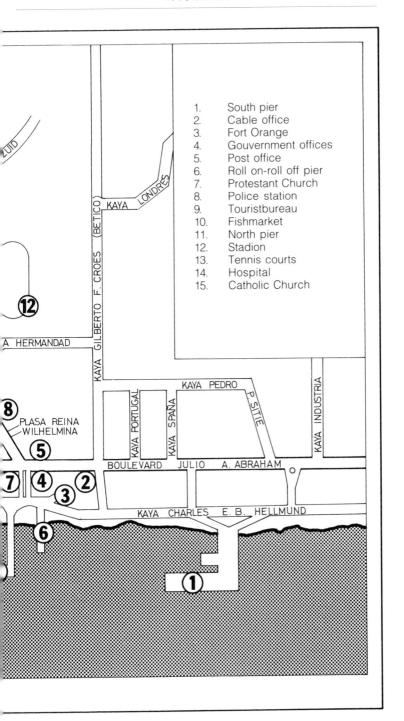

1.   South pier
2.   Cable office
3.   Fort Orange
4.   Gouvernment offices
5.   Post office
6.   Roll on-roll off pier
7.   Protestant Church
8.   Police station
9.   Touristbureau
10. Fishmarket
11. North pier
12. Stadion
13. Tennis courts
14. Hospital
15. Catholic Church

lendijk, but used to consist of two small village communities: North and South Nikiboko.

NORTH SALINA

Small village north of Kralendijk with approximately 1,500 inhabitants. The name means 'north of the saltpans'. Has also become a sort of outskirt of Kralendijk.

RINCÓN

This is the oldest village of Bonaire. The first Spaniards settled here in the beginning of the sixteenth century, because it was much safer to live inland and because the surroundings had a lush vegetation. The most important factor, however, was safety: from sea Rincón cannot be seen and pirates and other riffraff, if any, first had to go a long way in order to reach the settlement. Rincón lies in a valley and has about 2,000 inhabitants nowadays. In fact, it is the only real village on the island because it is the only place of residence not in the immediate vicinity of Kralendijk. It has all the characteristic features of a village. For instance, it has a village center with a church, St Ludovicus Bertrandus. It

Rincón, Bonaire's oldest village

is a friendly place with some cozy pubs (Amstelbar) and its location in the valley is magnificent. Certainly worth-while visiting!

TERRA CORÁ

Very small village with approximately 300 inhabitants, south-east of Kralendijk. The name means 'red soil' and the village came into existence about 1835 at the time of the slavery. Previously the slaves lived in Rincón, but after a revolt they were transported to this place. This slave village was located nearer to the saltpans and so the slaves could work longer, because the road they had to travel from here to the saltpans was considerably shorter.

CHAPTER 4

HOTELS

Tourism to Bonaire has slowly but surely come off the ground. Already in 1922 the first 'tourist' ships, the Baralt and the Merída moored at the wooden pier of Kralendijk. Cruise tourism only became popular in the second half of the 1960s and until today has formed an important source of income for the island. At least once a week in the high season (often on Friday) some fine cruise ship is to be admired at the pier in Kralendijk which was specially constructed for this purpose. Until the beginning of the fifties, however, Bonaire had no large scale accommodation facilities for tourists. This changed in 1952. In 1951 the Dutch merchant Lodewijk D. Gerharts, then living on the island, suggested to turn the former internment camp (see chapter 2 History), which had been vacant since 1947, into a hotel. At the time the rebuilding cost upwards of twenty-thousand Antillean guilders and in 1952 the first hotel on Bonaire opened, with the beautiful name Hotel Zeebad. However, after some years this name was changed into Flamingo Beach Club Hotel. The old, rebuilt wooden huts from the Second World War, rendered excellent services until 1973. In that year they were pulled down and on the same spot arose beautiful stone bungalows. The hotel has meanwhile had various owners, and nowadays it is owned by the Divi hotel group. This group also owns hotels on Aruba, Barbados, St Maarten and some other Caribbean islands. Recently the complex has been extended with a great many beautiful apartments, rented according to the so-called 'time share' principle. Meanwhile various hotels and apartment complexes have been erected on Bonaire. In 1962 the Bonaire Beach Hotel opened its doors - this hotel is located on the Playa Lechi and was built with development funds - and in 1969 Hotel Rochaline followed. Apart from these hotels the island has a number ot apartment complexes. One of these complexes, the Sorobon Beach Resort, is only open to naturists. In itself nothing special, but on many Caribbean islands it is not allowed to sun naked and this sheltered complex is an exception to this. So, on the island mainly apartments and no tall hotel buildings with 400 rooms under one roof, for the two bigger hotels (approximately 150 rooms) do not have more than two floors, although they do have a central reception desk and occasionally some facilities, such as a restaurant, swimming pool, shop(s). These two hotels, Bonaire Beach Hotel and the Flamingo Beach Hotel, also have each a casino. Of course these are also open to non-guests. So without trouble you can have dinner in the restaurant of another hotel or visit the casino there. Every week the hotels organize special theme-nights with shows, barbecues, and so on (for more information see chapter 6, Folklore and Festivities). Inquire about these activities at the hotels. Generally speaking, prices are reasonable and apart from an excellent meal, you are also treated to an attractive show. The more facilities a hotel has to offer, the higher the price you have to pay for a room. Therefore the bigger hotels are more expensive than the smaller. Below, an accommodation survey of Bonaire, subdivided into the more comfortable hotels and apartments. Prices mentioned (liable to change without previous warning, so always inquire in advance) are in American dollars, exclusive of 10% service tax and $ 2.30 per person per night room tax and are per night per room. Meals are not included in the price (breakfast sometimes is). Generally speaking, it is wiser and cheaper to book a trip via a travel agency from abroad. Then the price includes the ticket and the hotel, with or without breakfast. If you book the ticket and hotel separately, you often pay much more. So do not let yourself be put off by the sometimes high prices mentioned below. Inquire at your travel agency (see Practical information) about attractive travel offers. The high season runs from 16 December up to and including 15 April, the low season from 16 April up to and including 15 December.

BONAIRE BEACH HOTEL & CASINO
P.O. Box 34, Bonaire NA
tel. 8448 telex: 1291 HOBON
price indication:
low season: from $ 55.- to $ 120.-
high season: from $ 90.- to $ 170.-
Credit cards: AE, DC, V, MC, CB

Large hotel with 145 rooms (including 6 suites) located on the Playa Lechi (Papiamentu for 'milk beach') and at about one mile north of Kralendijk. The rooms are situated in a complex of two-floored buildings and surrounded by green plantation. The rooms have been redecorated recently and have all been provided with airconditioning, a bathroom

Playa Lechi near the Bonaire Beach Hotel

with shower and bath, telephone and a small balcony or patio. The hotel has two restaurants: the Neptune Dining Room and the Beach Hut Restaurant. Especially the latter restaurant has much atmosphere and a large number of special activities are organised there, such as theme-nights and folkloristic shows. Furthermore, the hotel has a casino, a mini-golfcourse, two open-air tennis courts (lit at night), a swimming pool, a boutique called Things Bonaire and a nice beach with deck chairs, sun beds and sun shades. At the beach various water sports can be practiced. Hotel guests, for instance, may free of charge use surfboards, small sunfish-sailing boats and paddle boats. Furthermore, there is a diving operation, the Bonaire Scuba Center. Daily between 6.00 and 7.00 p.m. there is Happy Hour - drinks and cocktails for half money and free snacks - in the Beach Hut. It is practical to know there are also babysitters present and that there is a laundry service. This makes this hotel very suited for people with children. In the hotel is a Budget office where you can rent a car. The hotel is being renovated to become a five star hotel.

DIVI FLAMINGO BEACH HOTEL & CASINO
(CLUB FLAMINGO)
Kralendijk, Bonaire NA
tel. 8285 or 8485 telex: 384 1293

price indication:
low season: from $ 55.- to $ 110.-
high season: from $ 75.- to $ 170.-
Credit cards: AE, DC, V, MC, CB

On the site where once the first hotel, called Zeebad, was built, one now finds this hotel complex, with 150 rooms. This informal hotel is located immediately on the sea at about half a mile from the center of Kralendijk. There are various types of rooms, varying from simple (Standard) to a bit more spacious (Deluxe), with a view of swimming pool or sea. All rooms have bath or shower, toilet and airconditioning. There are two swimming pools, a tennis court, a jacuzzi, two restaurants - Chibi Chibi restaurant and Calabas restaurant -, a bar outside, Flamingo's Nest, a casino (Flamingo Casino: open daily from 8.00 p.m., closed on Sunday) with next to it the Players Bar (happy hour from 9.00 to 10.00 p.m.), a boutique Ki Bo Ke Pakus, a photo shop Photo Bonaire, specialized in underwater photography and two dive shops, Dive Bonaire I and Dive Bonaire II. Furthermore, there is a Budget office, where cars can be rented, and excursions and flights booked. This hotel is especially popular because of its excellent diving facilities. In the restaurants there are weekly special activities, such as folkloristic shows. Moreover, there is a special Time-share project. Furthermore, this hotel has extensive provisions for the disabled. There are even dive courses for handicapped people.

CAPTAIN DON'S HABITAT & HAMLET
P.O. Box 88, Bonaire NA
tel. 8290 telex: 1926 HAMBO
price indication:
low season: from $ 18.- to $ 225.-
high season: from $ 25.- to $ 225.-
Credit cards: AE, DC, V, MC, CB

This is the domain of the famous Captain Don Stewart from America, the first man to recognize the great diving possibilities of Bonaire and to start the first dive operation on the island. The Habitat consists of nine apartments with two bedrooms, kitchen, bathroom and patio. The new Hamlet part consists of villas with airconditioning, kitchen, bathroom and veranda. There is a bar and restaurant, called Dolphin Club and a few evenings per week so-called theme-evenings are organised here. The diving operation situated here is called Aquaventure Dive Center. Dee Scarr as well here has its basis for its diving activities. At the moment a shopping arcade and a new restaurant are under construction.

HOTEL ROCHALINE
P.O. Box 27, Kralendijk, Bonaire NA
tel. 8286 or 8822 telex: 1187
price indication:
low season: from $ 36.- to $ 48.-
high season: from $ 36.- to $ 48.-
Credit cards: AE, DC, V, MC, CB

This is a small hotel in the center of Kralendijk opposite the fish market, with 20 simple rooms with airconditioning.
The hotel has a good restaurant, called Lisboa Terrace. Thishotel has no diving facilities, but one can use, for instance, the nearby Dive Inn.

SOROBON BEACH RESORT
P.O. Box 14, Bonaire NA
tel. 8080 telex: 1280 BON TRAD
price indication:
low season: from $ 50.- to $ 90.-
high season: from $ 75.- to $ 125.-
Credit cards: AE, DC, V, MC, CB

This hotel, the only one located on the east coast of Bonaire, is exclusively open to naturists. The complex is made up of seventeen wooden apartments on the beach of and with a view of Lac. There are apartments with one and with two bedrooms, and studios with kitchenette. They all have a shower or bath. For naturists in search of quiet this hotel is ideal. There is a small shop where food and drinks can be bought and there is a small restaurant (only for guests). There is a daily service between the hotel and Kralendijk for guests who do not have transport of their own. Informal atmosphere. New apartments are being built, as well as a tennis court. For diving people can go to Dive Inn in Kralendijk.

BACHELOR'S BEACH APARTMENTS
P.O. Box 170, Belnem 28, Bonaire NA
tel. 8073
price indication:
low season : from $ 473.- to $ 630.- per week
high season: from $ 500.- to $ 700.- per week
Credit cards: AE, DC, V, MC, CB

Three apartments located south of Kralendijk and the airport, along the road to the saltpans and the Salt Lake. They are situated on the sea and all three have airconditioning, kitchen, bathroom and patio. The apartment complex has a pier, giving access to the sea.

BONAIRE BEACH BUNGALOWS
P.O. Box 155, Bonaire NA
tel. 8585 or 8581
price indication:
low season: from $ 440.- to $ 495.- per week
high season: from $ 520.- to $ 570.- per week
Credit cards: AE, DC, V, MC, CB

Six apartments located on the sea south of Kralendijk and the airport, along the road to the saltpans and the Salt Lake. The apartments are each made up of two bedrooms, a fully fitted kitchen, bathroom and patio.

GOLDEN TULIP BONAIRE SUNSET INN & VILLAS
P.O. Box 115, Bonaire NA
tel. 8291, 8300 or 8400 telex: 1280 BTC NA, telefax: (5997) 8865price indication:
low season: from $ 35.- to $ 150.-
high season: from $ 35.- to $ 180.-
Credit cards: AE, DC, V, MC, CB

Under this name a great variety of one-room and double-room apartments and two- three- and five-room houses are offered on various locations. They are partly situated near the center of Kralendijk and partly south of the airport. All apartments and houses are completely furnished, provided with linen and fully fitted kitchen (including a food-processor and a microwave oven), airconditioning, telephone, bathroom, 12 channel cable-TV's (one in the living room and one in the bedroom(s)) and a weekly 'maid-service'. If necessary, a baby sitter is available. For diving, one can appeal to Bruce Bowker of Carib Inn, or Anton van de Heetkamp of Dive Inn.

BUDDY'S DIVE RESORT
P.O. Box 231, Bonaire NA
tel. 8065 or 8647 telex: 1200 INPO
price indication:
low season: from $ 45.- to $ 65.-
high season: from $ 45.- to $ 85.-
Credit cards: AE, DC, V, MC, CB

Twenty apartments, ten of which are located opposite the Bonaire Beach Hotel and the marina, and ten which have been built recently, between Sand Dollar and Captain Don Habitat. The apartments are completely furnished and have a kitchen, bathroom, airconditioning and patio. Buddy's Watersports Center takes care of the water sport activities here. These apartments are sometimes offered under the name Carabella Bungalows. There are expansion plans: by 1990 they will have the disposal of 144 bungalows/apartments.

CARIB INN
P.O. Box 68, Bonaire NA
tel. 8819
price indication:
low season: from $ 39.- to $ 89.-
high season: from $ 49.- to $ 115.-
Credit cards: AE, DC, V, MC, CB

Small complex, located next to the Flamingo Beach Hotel, consisting of ten rooms and three apartments. The rooms and apartments are provided with airconditioning, cable TV, a bathroom, patio, and on weekdays there is 'maid service', so that people do not have to do everything themselves. The apartments also have a kitchenette. The complex is located on the sea and there is a small freshwater swimming pool. They also have a well-equipped diving operation, under the management of Bruce Bowker. When booking, a $ 125.- deposit should be paid.

SAND DOLLAR CONDOMINIUMS & BEACH CLUB
P.O. Box 175, Bonaire NA
tel. 8738
price indication:
low season: from $ 98.- to $ 170.-
high season: from $ 98.- to $ 170.-
Credit cards: AE, DC, V, MC, CB

Magnificent project, at the moment consisting of 84 luxurious apartments, with one, two or three bedrooms, fully fitted kitchen, balcony with view of the sea, airconditioning, bathroom, telephone, TV, etc. One of the most luxurious apartment complex of the whole island. The attractive open-air restaurant Green Parrot is located on the coast and here you also find André Nahr's Sand Dollar Dive & Photo Shop. This diving operation is very good. A number of new expansions is forthcoming, including a great many new apartments, a shopping-arcade, tennis courts, a health club and a second restaurant.

FINALLY.....

Apart from the existing hotels and apartments mentioned above, there are plans to build a number of new complexes. For instance there are advanced plans for the building of a complex of apartments near the lighthouse south of Kralendijk, called Lighthouse Beach Resort. Furthermore, near Belnem a complex of 25 'time-share' villas will be built as an expansion of Sunset Villas. Moreover there are plans to build a number of villas called Lagun Villas, near the lagoon on the east coast of the island. At the time of the compilation of this travelers' handbook, these projects were still in a very premature stage and maybe they will never be realized, or maybe they have finished building meanwhile and the villas are ready. For more information, inquire at the Bonaire Tourist Board, Kaya Grandi 3, Kralendijk, tel. 8322 or 8649.

CHAPTER 5

FOOD AND DRINKS

THE ANTILLEAN KITCHEN

Just like the population, the language and the music and dance, Antillean cooking is the result of the amalgamation of different peoples and cultures. The so-called Kushina Krioyo or the Creole kitchen determines to a great extent the manner and ways of cooking on Bonaire. Antillean cooking bears a strong resemblance to that of the other Caribbean islands and the continent of South America, especially to the kitchen of Venezuela. Considering the proximity of this country on the South American mainland, this is not surprising. The fact that there are many points in common with the other Caribbean islands, is related to the colonial past, when the islands changed owner with the regularity of clockwork, and the local population was consequently confronted with various cultures and ways of cooking. Apart from this, the business contacts among the islands have contributed to the development of typically Creole food. For the origin of this characteristic cuisine, we must go back to the times prior to the Spaniards. The original inhabitants of the islands, the Indians, provided themselves with food by means of hunting, catching fish and a primitive form of agriculture. The main agricultural products of that early period were maize and brown beans, two ingredients still playing an important part in the current local cuisine. Also peanuts, sweet potatoes and cocoa were grown on a small scale. The meat people ate, was mainly turkey, iguana and duck. Fish and testaceans were abundantly to be found in the surrounding waters, so these were used as well. With the arrival of the Spaniards, the local population was introduced to sugar, salt, lard, lemon, olives, etc. For their part, the Spaniards came to know many new dishes and ingredients of the local Indian population. With the arrival of the Dutch in the beginning of the seventeenth century a number of other products and ingredients was added, such as cheese and bacon. The most important contribution to the development of Creole cooking comes, however, from the black slaves, in large numbers imported from Africa. They had bananas with them, for instance, which are still important in the local cuisine, and they had a number of cooking habits which, though modernized, still characterize Antillean cooking. They introduced, for instance, funchi, a porridge of flour and later maize. Cooking in banana leaves also stems from the African slaves. The influence of the black slaves on the local cuisine has been so great, because the majority of the people at the time consisted of slaves and they were not really served the best food. Fresh meat or fish were not on the daily menu. Dried fish, funchi, turnips and sweet potatoes were the main constituents. Only after the abolition of slavery, leaf vegetables such as spinach and lettuce were introduced. Another important aspect is formed by the climatic circumstances of the islands. It is extremely dry there, and consequently growing vegetables and such is hardly possible, so that fresh vegetables, fruit and other food have to be imported from elsewhere. Especially Venezuela plays an important part in this.For many years people from Venezuela have crossed the strait that separates Bonaire from Venezuela, in so-called small barks, and have offered their fresh merchandise on the market of Kralendijk. During the last few decades, food customs have been subject to changes again under the influence of tourism, especially from the United States and Canada.

Authentic

In spite of the many influences from outside there is still a number of Antillean dishes that more or less deserve the designation 'authentic'. A typically Antillean dish is still Funchi, consisting of maize-semolina, water, salt and butter. It is a kind of porridge that, with a small dollop of butter, takes the place of our rice or potatoes in the entree. Occasionally this dish is 'decorated' with sugar, cheese or fried banana. Banana, cooked or fried (Banana Hasà), takes a prominent position on the Antillean's menu. The so-called Stobà dishes are favorites as well. These are stews with for a basis goat's flesh or mutton mixed with vegetables and spices. There are many variations and such a dish is often a complete meal in itself. Considering the location of the islands, surrounded by waters much swarming with fish, it will be obvious that fish takes an important place on the daily menu of the Antillean. In fact, people eat more fish than meat. Around Bonaire, located on the continental shelf of South America and separated from South America in the south and west by water, especially many reef fish are caught, for instance the Great Barracuda, Red Snappers, groupers and Mulatos (Wahoo). Lobsters and shrimps are very popular. Regarding meat, especially goat's flesh used to be popular. Nowadays people eat more chicken and pork as a rule. Beef is found less often in authentic Antillean cooking. The reason is obvious: the weather conditions are far from ideal for raising cattle, whereas goats, sheep, pigs and chickens make less demands concerning their food. The vast majority of the meat consumed on these islands nowadays, is imported from abroad.

Fruit often is the basis for local drinks. Popular for instance is Awa di Sorsaka, a drink composed of the juice of the soursop fruit (having a dark green rind and soft prickles, white pulp and black stones), ice cubes, sugar, milk and (sometimes) cinnamon and vanilla. On hot days - which are numerous here - this is an excellent thirst-quencher.

Meals

As a rule the Antillean has the principal meal in the afternoon; then there is an extensive dinner with soup and fish or meat with funchi. Soup is very popular as a main meal. In that case, it is a hearty soup, containing meat, fish or fruit as main ingredient. Soppi di Banana, for instance, is a soup containing banana, Soppi di Cabritu is goat's flesh soup, Soppi di Galinja is chicken soup and Soppi di Pisca is fish soup. Generally speaking, breakfast is simple: a cup of coffee or tea and one or two sandwiches, with or without egg or something like that. In the evening one may have dinner again, but usually only some sandwiches with a small snack are taken, for instance a Pastechi, a patty filled with meat or fish. Long after sunset people often indulge in local snacks such as Empanadas (patties of maize-semolina filled with meat, chicken or fish) and Cala (a kind of croquette made of strongly spiced and ground beans: Boonchi Wowo Pretoe - small white beans with black 'eyes'). These are very popular among the local population. However, it is becoming more and more difficult to point out what dishes are authentically Antillean and what not. The influences from outside are so great that you can hardly speak of Antillean cooking. Only the handful of dishes mentioned above more or less deserve the designation 'authentic'. Not only as far as its people, language and culture are concerned Bonaire is a melting pot, in the culinary field as well influences from all directions are found. Nevertheless the Antillean is a true gourmet and wise enough to adopt only those dishes that are really delicious and special. The result is that modern Antillean cooking is a mixture of all kinds of national and foreign dishes, each of which is nevertheless very tasty. It is recommendable to try some of these dishes, for instance in one of the restaurants mentioned below. In this way you get to know and appreciate Bonaire and its population still better. When doing so especially do not forget the Antillean saying: 'A full stomach goes hand in hand with a happy heart.' Enjoy your meal!

Bonairean cooking

There is not much difference between the cooking of Curaçao and that of Bonaire. Some minor distinctions are that on Bonaire people as a rule eat more goat's meat than on Curaçao. After slaughtering the goat, part of the meat is salted and dried in the sun. This is later used in dishes. Part of the goat's meat is also used for stews, roasts and soups. Head, hooves, stomach, kidneys, liver, heart and spleen are cooked to a nourishing soup or eaten stewed. A tradition on Bonaire is to have a pancake on Good Friday, made of buttermilk and sorghum flour. For the rest, Bonairean cooking is not different from Antillean cooking in general.

RESTAURANTS

The number of restaurants on Bonaire is limited. The majority is to be found in the few hotels on the island. Below you find a survey of the main restaurants. The restaurants marked with an asterisk are definitely worth a visit. Of each restaurant is given in succession: the address, the telephone number, opening times, the type of cooking, the possibility to pay with credit cards and if so, what cards are accepted, and finally an indication regarding the price level. The latter indicates the prices of the restaurants in relation to those of the others.

Beach Hut
Bonaire Beach Hotel
tel. 8448
Breakfast, Lunch & Dinner (7.00 a.m. - 10.30 p.m.)
Cooking: International
Credit cards: AE, MC, DC, V Price level: moderate

The Beach Hut is part of the Bonaire Beach Hotel and located on the Playa Lechi beach. It is a semi open-air restaurant with a thatched roof, a spacious beachbar and many tables. Furthermore, there is a dance-floor. It is open practically all day. Apart from having breakfast, you can also have excellent lunch and dinner here. For lunch the menu offers sandwiches, salads and an occasional fish-dish. Especially for the children there is the 'Kid's Corner'. For dinner, various theme-nights and folkloristic shows are organised here. On Monday night, for instance, there is a Steak Night à la Carte, on Tuesday night an Indonesian Night, on Wednesday night a Casino Dinner à la Carte, Thursday night a Barbecue Night, on Friday night a Seafood Festival à la Carte and on Saturday night Bonairean Night with a folkloristic show. On Sunday there is a Champagne Brunch in the afternoon and a Welcome to the Island Bar-becue at night. Many of these evenings there is 'live' enter-tainment. Happy Hour is daily from 6.00 - 7.00 p.m. and is very cozy here. The drinks can be ordered for half price and snacks are served free of charge. Over a delicious cocktail you can watch a magnificent sunset. Recommend-ed!

Beefeater Restaurant *
Kaya Grandi 12, Kralendijk
tel. 8081 or 8773
Dinner: (6.30 - 11.00 p.m.), closed on Sunday
Cooking: International, Fish
Credit cards: AE, DC, V, MC
Price level: moderate

This restaurant is located in the center of Kralendijk, imme-diately opposite the Bonaire Tourist Board Office in a typi-cally Bonairean yellow house. It has a small gallery in front, with the front door in the middle. It is a small intimate restau-rant, consisting of three small rooms with about 10 tables in all. At the back, to the right, in a special room is the bar. The walls are half covered with laths and above these are some paintings, for instance showing the Big Ben in London and some sea views. The menu card is varied and prices are indicated in Antillean guilders. Some dishes on the menu are: entrees: Shrimp Cocktail, Melon; soups: French Onion soup, Bouillabaisse in the Bonairean way; main dishes: Roasted Salmon, T-bone Steak. Specialties here are the Steak- and Fish dishes. The restaurant is airconditioned.

Bistro Des Amis *
Kaya L.D. Gerharts 4, Kralendijk
tel. 8003 or 8700
Dinner (6.30 - 11.00 p.m.), closed on Sunday
Cooking: French
Credit cards: AE, MC, V, DC
Price level: expensive

No doubt this is the most stylish as well as the best restaurant of the island. This may already be observed at the entrance with its beautiful door. After entering you see a large bar with about 20 seats and on the bar is an antique gramophone. The wall behind the bar is full with wine bottles. Along the wall there are about seven laid tables with table covers in light colors and with wooden chairs. There are paintings, shaded lamps and Delft blue plates on the wall. Near the entrance is a piano, at which everyone who feels like it, can sit down and play. The menu looks excellent and contains for instance the following dishes: entrees: Cocktail de Crevettes, soups: French Onion soup; fish dishes: Fish of the day, Lobstertail; meat dishes: Tournedos with four sorts of peppers and for dessert Cheese and the Dessert-trolley. The cooking is good and mainly fresh ingredients are used. The wine card is very extensive, including White Bourgogne, Loire wine, Macon A.C., Pouilly Fumé A.C., Red Bordeaux, Red Bourgogne, Beaujolais, Côte du Rhone, Red Provence, White Bordeaux. All in all a restaurant with atmosphere and a touch of Paris. This impression is strengthened by a small dance-floor at the back, to the right, which allows one to have a 'diner-dansant' here. Booking recommended.

Calabas Restaurant
Flamingo Beach Hotel, Kralendijk
tel. 8285 or 8485
Breakfast, Lunch & Dinner (7.00 a.m. - 10.00 p.m.)
Cooking: International
Credit cards: AE, DC, MC, V
Price level: moderate

This restaurant is part of the Flamingo Beach Hotel and located on the sea. It is open at practically all hours of the day, for breakfast, lunch and dinner. For lunch you can have dishes such as soups, salads, sandwiches and an occasional fish-dish. There is a limited menu for dinner. A choice can be made out of about seven main dishes, such as Chicken, Steak, Catch of the Day, etc. Furthermore, there are special theme-evenings: every Tuesday night, for instance, there is an Indonesian Buffet, every Thursday night a Seafood Festival, and on Sunday afternoon a Sunday Brunch and at night a Roastbeef Buffet. Twice a week there is a folkloristic performance during dinner. On this occasion people dance in Bonairean costumes to local music. The tables and chairs in the restaurant are white, on the tables are red cloths and in the evening there are wax lights on the tables. There is a nice atmosphere. The big bar is to be found immediately behind the entrance.

Capricon Bar & Restaurant
Boulevard J.A. Abraham 12
tel. 8178
Breakfast, Lunch & Dinner (7.00 a.m.- 12.00 p.m. or 2.00 a.m.)
Cooking: International, Antillean
Credit cards: none
Price level: inexpensive

Small intimate restaurant with about seven tables. There is a small dancefloor in the right corner. French and Bonairean music is played here. Especially popular among the local population. Here you can also have authentic Antillean dishes.

Dolphin Club
Kaya Gov. Debrot 103
tel. 8290
Breakfast, Lunch & Dinner (7.30 a.m. - 9.30 p.m.)
Cooking: International, Antillean
Credit cards: V, MC
Price level: moderate

Open-air restaurant with a nice view of the sea. The interior consists of simple wooden tables and chairs. The quality of the cooking is fine. Here as well special theme-nights are organised. On Tuesday night, for instance, there is a Barbecue Night with open grill dishes and on Thursday night there is Tex Mex Nite with Mexican dishes and Captain Don Stewart behind the bar, mixing hearty tequilas. This bar is located next to the restaurant (Happy Hour from 5.00 to 6.00 p.m.) and has some cozy nooks and a 'games corner'. On the wall there are all kinds of newspaper and magazine clippings about the famous Captain Don. Informal atmosphere.

Chibi Chibi Restaurant
Flamingo Beach Hotel, Kralendijk
tel. 8285 or 8485
Dinner (6.00 - 10.00 p.m.)
Cooking: International
Credit cards: AE, DC, MC, V
Price level: expensive

This restaurant belongs to the Flamingo Beach Hotel and is located in a wooden hut, partly above the water and open on all sides. It has two floors and a roof. Apart from the sea wind a large number of fans provide cooling. Practically from every seat you have a nice view of the sea. The menu here contains main dishes such as: Lobster, Catch of the Day, Shrimp Scampi, Fettuccine Flamingo, Filet Mignon, etc. The Calabas restaurant and the Chibi Chibi restaurant have the same wine card, with French, German, Portuguese and Spanish wines. Some wines are: Gewürztraminer, Pouilly Fumé, Blanc de Blanc, Soave. Apart from a bottle of wine you can also order a glass, a half or a whole decanter of wine. A very attractive restaurant for an open-air dinner.

Le Chic Cocktails & Cuisine
Kaya Charles E.B. Hellmund 5
tel. 8617
Dinner (5.00 - 12.00 p.m.), closed on Tuesday
Cooking: French, International
Credit cards: AE Price level: expensive

The latest acquisition in the culinary field on the island. Fashionable interior with white walls and pastel green accents and modern paintings. These shades can also be found in the upholstery of the cane chairs. There is a small bar with cocktails as specialty of the house. Here you can choose out of over thirty different cocktails with exotic names, such as 'Flying Kangeroo', 'Juicy Lucy', 'Erotic Lady', 'Golden Dream', etc. Very enjoyable. The menu contains three cold and three warm entrees, three soups, a salad, eight main dishes, the majority of which have fish, and four desserts. Some fish dishes: Soufflé de Sole Royale, Homard Grillé au Citron en Poisson du Jour. The cooking has a touch of nouvelle cuisine, however without the finesse for which this style of cooking became so famous. The wine card is rather limited with fourteen wines. There is a terrace with about 20 seats where you can have an appetizer or one of the many cocktails. Booking (especially in the weekend) is desirable.

China Garden Restaurant & Bar*
Kaya Grandi 47, Kralendijk
tel. 8480
Lunch & Dinner (11.30 a.m.- 2.00 p.m. and 4.00 - 10.00 p.m.), closed on Tuesday
Cooking: Chinese, International, Indian, Antillean
Credit cards: DC, AE, V, MC

Price level: moderate

This Chinese restaurant in the center of Kralendijk is located in a beautifully restored Bonairean house. At the entrance is a big red Chinese drum. After entering you come into the part of the house where the bar is. Do not think this is the restaurant, but follow the two signs to the dining-room. On arrival there, a lady with the menu will show you the way. The restaurant has airconditioning and accommodates about 60 guests. The tables are neatly laid with the plates upside down on the tables. On the walls there are some cane shaded lamps and some cudweeds. Furthermore there is a separate room for private dinners. Some suggestions for the menu are: China Garden Special, Karkó (conch) in Black Bean Sauce and Nasi Goreng Special. Moreover the menu - containing well over 200 dishes! - has some curry dishes, for instance Curry Shrimp and Curry Goat. There is also a take-out service.

China Nobo Restaurant & Bar
Kaya Nikiboko 4
tel. 8981
Lunch & Dinner (11.30 a.m. - 2.30 p.m. and 4.30 - 12.00 p.m.), closed on Tuesday
Cooking: Chinese, Antillean
Credit cards: none
Price level: inexpensive

Simple Chinese restaurant. At the entrance you will find to the left the restaurant section with six tables. It all looks neat. On the wall there are Chinese lanterns. To the right is a small bar with five stools. The menu has about 100 dishes, mainly based on Cantonese cooking. There is also a take-out service. Especially popular among the local population.

Den Laman Aquarium Bar & Restaurant *
Kaya Gov. Debrot Road (between Hotel Bonaire Beach and Sand Dollar Beach)
tel. 8955
Dinner (6.00 - 11.00 p.m.), closed on Tuesday
Cooking: Fish, Antillean, International
Credit cards: AE, MC, V, DC
Price level: moderate

This restaurant has a remarkable interior. After entering you see to the left a wooden boat, serving as a bar. The restaurant has about 14 wooden tables, surrounded by wooden chairs with blue artificial leather covering. Most remarkable are the two walls in which are big aquaria, containing a large variety of fish including a shark, turtles, morays and reef fish. The other two walls display all kinds of fish ornaments. A fish-shaped blackboard mentions the Catch of the Day. Behind the restaurant, on the seaside, is a large bar with also a big aquarium, in which lobsters are swimming. The menu has a large variety of fish, including grouper, red snapper, lobster, etc. The card mentions two meat dishes as well. The specialties here are: Lobster Cocktail, Turtle Steak and Whole Snapper. Booking recommended!

Egretta Bar & Restaurant
Lac Sorobon
tel. none
Breakfast, Lunch & Dinner (11.00 a.m. - 11.00 p.m.), closed on Monday
Cooking: International
Credit cards: none
Price level: moderate

This intimate restaurant is near the beautiful lagoon of Lac. At the front door there are two colorful parrots. After entering the restaurant, you will find the bar to the right and the kitchen behind. The restaurant section is to the left and has about nine tables. The restaurant is furnished attractively with, for instance, an antique oak book case, a big bar and a glass sideboard, in which chinaware and such is displayed. There are many shaded lamps and paintings. The whole has a homey atmosphere. On the menu you find dishes such as Shrimp cocktail, Grouper, Conch and T-bone steak. There is a nice wine card with French wines.

Great China Restaurant *
Kaya Grandi 39, Kralendijk
tel. 8886Lunch & Dinner (11.00 a.m. - 11.00 p.m.), closed on Monday
Cooking: Chinese
Credit cards: V
Price level: moderate

This Chinese restaurant located in the center of Kralendijk is especially popular among the local population. You immediately enter the bar, and to the right is the small restaurant. It looks a bit cheerless due to the fluorescent lighting. There are about seven tables covered in red (35 persons). There is airconditioning. The entrance is on the Kaya Kórsow. The walls are half covered with laths. Limited, but good wine card. The atmosphere may not be optimum, but the food is good.

Green Parrot *
Sand Dollar Beach Club
tel. 8738
Breakfast, Lunch & Dinner (7.30 a.m. - 11.00 p.m., on Saturday until 12.00 p.m.), closed on Monday
Cooking: International
Credit cards: AE, DC, V, MC
Price level: moderate

This semi open-air restaurant of the Sand Dollar Condominium & Beach Club is located by the sea and has about 20 cane tables and chairs with green cushions. Big fans hang from the ceiling. After entering you find the bar to the left and the kitchen behind. Above the bar are mahogany cabinets. Happy Hour is from 5.00 - 7.00 p.m. here. Ask for the specialty called Lora Berde (a greenish cocktail containing brandy among other things). Each Saturday night they organise a Barbecue Night with 'live' music. Every day you can have breakfast, lunch and dinner. Lunch card dishes (for instance, Hamburgers and Sandwiches) may be ordered in the evening as well. You are not obliged to order from the dinner menu. The latter mentions dishes such as Shrimps, Fresh fish, cooked or fried, U.S. Sirloin Steak, Filet Mignon. Moreover you can choose out of five kinds of wine. Informal atmosphere and efficient service.

Jos's Bar & Restaurant
Kaya Korona 79
tel. 4232
Lunch & Dinner (no fixed opening times)
Cooking: Chinese, International
Credit cards: none
Price level: inexpensive

Small restaurant with a bar with four stools and only three tables. Furthermore there is an old juke-box in the room. The whole is simple but neat. The menu contains various fish dishes, soups, omelets, chicken with rice, beef with rice. Especially popular among the local population.

Lisboa Terrace *
Hotel Rochaline, Kralendijk
tel. 8286 or 8822

Breakfast, Lunch & Dinner (7.30 a.m. - 11.00 p.m.)
Cooking: International, Fish
Credit cards: DC, AE, V, MC
Price level: moderate

Exactly opposite the fish market in the center of Kralendijk is Hotel Rochaline. The entrance of this semi open-air restaurant is on the seaside. The restaurant section has about 15 tables with plastic chairs. When you go towards the hotel entrance, you will find the bar behind the restaurant as well, to the left. It is a wooden bar, decorated with blue and yellow tiles. In the restaurant Ipiranga wicker bottles hang from the ceiling. The card mentions fish dishes and steaks, but also dishes such as Lasagna. Some fish dishes are: Lobster, Shrimps prepared in different ways, Grouper, Catch of the Day, etc. The wine of the house is Vino Verde. This restaurant is simple but neat and has an informal atmosphere. Fish is its specialty.

Mona Lisa Bar & Restaurant *
Kaya Grandi 15, Kralendijk
tel. 8718
Breakfast, Lunch & Dinner (11.00 a.m. - 2.00 or 3.00 a.m.), closed on Sunday
Cooking: International, Fish
Credit cards: none
Price level: moderate

Cozy bar (kind of a pub) and restaurant with four tables in the bar. The walls are half covered with wood and painted red and green. There are fans on the ceiling, because there is no airconditioning. Behind the bar on a large winerack are the wine bottles and other alcoholic liquors. There is an old-fashioned telephone. Over the bar hang five nice lamps and there are some oil-lamps (nowadays on electricity) on the bar. In the bar there is a 'Small card', containing dishes such as: various omelets, slices of bread with ham or cold meat and a fried egg on top, German rumpsteak and Chili Con Carne. The restaurant section is left of the entrance and has about eight tables. Here as well there are fans on the ceiling (no airconditioning). The restaurant looks somewhat like a living room because of the many paintings on the wall. The card contains four cold and four hot entrees and about 10 main dishes, including Hungarian Goulash, Tournedos Stroganoff and Fish of the Day à la Creole. Informal atmosphere.

The Rendez-Vous *
Kaya L.D. Gerharts 3, Kralendijk
tel. 8454
Lunch & Dinner (6.00 - 11.00 p.m.), closed on Tuesday
Cooking: International, Fish
Credit cards: AE, V, MC
Price level: moderate

In the evening this restaurant has a cozily-lit veranda with seven tables on which wax lights are put. The tables here are covered with brown cloths. Inside is a large bar with high stools. In this room are furthermore about six tables with small red lamps (paraffin) on them. Behind the bar a wall with laths. Moreover there are many beautiful pictures of Bonaire on the wall. There is airconditioning, but there are big fans as well. You can have delicious espresso coffee here and atmospheric background music is played. The menu contains many fish dishes such as Catch of the Day, Garlic Shrimps, Shrimp and Conchplatter, but also meat dishes such as Wiener Schnitzel, Tenderloin Steak and a local meat dish called Keshi Yena (grilled chicken with vegetables and raisins, covered with processed Dutch cheese). Entrees are, for instance, Escargots Bourguignonne and Avocado Shrimp cocktail. The card contains also some vegetarian dishes, Spaghetti Milanesa and small dishes such as omelets and salads. The wine card has apart from Champagne (Veuve Cliquot), some white wines such as Chablis A.C., Sancerre A.C. and Gewürztraminer, and red wines such as St. Emilion A.C. and Rioja Fuasatine V.A.C.. Especially late at night it is very cozy here. Recommended!

Zeezicht Bar & Restaurant *
Kaya Curaçao 1, Kralendijk
tel. 8434
Breakfast, Lunch & Dinner (8.30 a.m. - 11.00 p.m.)
Cooking: Fish
Credit cards: AE, DC, V, MC
Price level: expensive

This restaurant is located by the sea and has a magnificent view. It is furnished atmospherically, has a tiled floor inside, tables laid in red and chairs, the seats and backs of which have goat hides. The section inside has six tables and on the terrace are another ten tables. Furthermore there is a large bar inside, decorated with fish nets and all kinds of shipping attributes. Over the bar hang three lamps made of Karkós. On the first floor of the building is another large room with 60 tables and a dancefloor, called 'Pirate House'. In the weekend (in high season) you can dance here from around 11.00 p.m. The menu shows a picture of a boat (Endeuver), built by the grandfather of the present proprietress. Specialties on the card are: Zeezicht Special I, consisting of sea view soup, fresh fish, deep-fried banana and a dessert; Zeezicht Special II, consisting of among other things conch, shrimp, fish, octopus, lobster; Nasi Goreng Special and furthermore the card has many fish dishes such as Stewed Conch, Curry Conch, Grilled Conch, Lobster and meat dishes such as U.S. Sirloin Steak and T-bone Steak. There is a separate lunch and breakfast menu. No airconditioning but fans. Do pay this restaurant a visit and have dinner on the atmospherically lit terrace. Recommended!

CHAPTER 6

SPORTS, SHOPPING, FOLKLORE, FESTIVITIES AND GOING OUT

SPORTS

The possibilities to practice some (water)sport on Bonaire are legion. Bonaire is ideal for the water sportsman and especially for the lovers of underwater sports - the divers among us - it is a true paradise! In this chapter a survey of all sports that can be practiced on Bonaire, with of course much, very much attention for diving. First the addresses of the firms that are responsible for the greater part of the (water)sports activities on Bonaire:

Aquaventure Dive Center, P.O. Box 88, Bonaire NA, tel. 8290, telex: 1926 HAMCO;
Bonaire Scuba Center, P.O. Box 106, Bonaire NA, tel. 8978, telex: 1291 HOBON;
Buddy's Watersports, P.O. Box 231, Bonaire NA, tel. 8647 or 8065, telex: 1200 INPO;
Carib Inn Dive Shop, P.O. Box 68, Bonaire NA, tel. 8819;
Dee Scarr's 'Touch the Sea', P.O. Box 369, Bonaire NA, tel. 8529;
Ocean Breeze Watersports, Bonaire Beach Hotel, tel. 8978;
Peter Hughes Dive Bonaire, Kralendijk, Bonaire NA, tel. 8285;
The Dive Inn, Kaya C.E.B. Hellmund 27, Bonaire NA, tel. 8761, telex: 1280 BON TRAD;
Sand Dollar Dive & Photo, P.O. Box 175, Bonaire NA, tel. 8738.

BOAT PADDLING

Exploring the Caribbean Sea while boat paddling. At Ocean-breeze Watersports on the beach near the Bonaire Beach

Hotel (tel. 8978) you can rent a paddle-boat at $ 20.- per half hour and at $ 30.- per hour.

BRIDGE

At the local bridgeclub Ups and Downs tourists are welcome to come and play along. The enrollment fee is $ 4.- a time for two persons. For the drinks you have to pay yourself. If you want to participate in a bridge-drive, you have to pay $ 17.- the two. This price includes the drinks. Generally the weekly bridge night is Tuesday night. The competitions start at 7.30 p.m. You have to be there 7.20 p.m. at the latest. Enrolling at the latest 2.00 p.m. the day before. The address of the bridgeclub Ups and Downs is Boulevard J.A. Abraham 29, Kralendijk (close to the Flamingo Beach Hotel). For entering and for more information: tel. 8136.

CANOEING

Lovers of canoeing can rent a canoe at Oceanbreeze Watersports on the beach near the Bonaire Beach Hotel. Prices per half hour: $ 20.- and per hour: $ 30.-.

CYCLING

Especially during the day the temperature on Bonaire is not exactly suitable for a strenuous cycling tour, but if you cannot resist the temptation to get on the saddle, there is a possibility to hire a bicycle and to make a cycling tour. In general the roads on the south-side of the island are flat. At nearly every hotel you can hire a bicycle. The price is $ 5.- a day. However, you have to pay a $ 100.- deposit per bicycle. There are special weekly rates. At the Budget Office you can rent a battery-powered moped - bicycles with a light motor - at $ 14.- a day or $ 70.- a week.

DEEP SEA FISHING

Deep-sea fishing is possible on Bonaire. The fish you can catch are numerous: Barracuda, the White or Blue Marlin, Wahoo, Bonito, Amberjack, Sailfish, Kingfish and Tuna are some of the fish species in which the deeper waters around Bonaire abound. You can hire specially equipped charter boats for a whole day or half a day. It makes no difference whether or not you are an experienced deep-sea fisher, because captain and crew will gladly show you all aspects of this fascinating sport. Below a few addresses where you can rent a charter boat, with price indications. Prices often apply per boat and do not depend on the number of persons (there is a maximum, however).

Piscatur Fishing Charters
Playa Pabao, Kralendijk
tel. 8774
Price indications:
Half a day small boat (15 ft) for max. 2 persons: $ 95.-
Whole day small boat (15 ft) for max. 2 persons: $ 150.-
Half a day big boat (24 ft) for max. 5 persons: $ 225.-
Whole day big boat (24 ft) for max. 5 persons: $ 350.-
Rods are also hired out: $ 5.- to $ 7.- per day or $ 25.- per week. The office is open from 8.30 to 12.00 a.m. and from 2.30 to 6.00 p.m.

Karel Watersports
Kaya J.N.E. Craane, Kralendijk
tel. 8434
Half a day with the boat Wave Killer (40 ft) with captain Kees Visser (min. 2 persons): $ 60.- including coffee and sandwiches.

The Dive Inn
(Kaya C.E.B. Hellmund 27, Kralendijk, tel. 8761) and Flamingo Beach Hotel (Kralendijk, tel. 8285) organise deep-sea fishing trips as well. Inquire at the reception desk of your hotel, or at the Bonaire Tourist Board Office, Kaya Grandi 3, Kralendijk (tel. 8322 or 8649) about the possibilities.

DIVING

The waters around Bonaire are a true paradise and belong to the most beautiful spots of the world for deep-sea divers. The underwater scenery is highly fascinating and a number of wrecked ships make diving very adventurous. The view under water is excellent and the temperature of the water is so pleasant that diving suits are often not needed. Wearing a T-shirt you can dive without trouble. Bonaire has a large number of excellent diving spots, varying in depth from 15 to 150 feet. There are some very interesting wrecks. Besides, there are enchanting coral reefs certainly worth visit-

The first diving lesson in the swimming pool

ing. Both experienced divers and beginners can enjoy themselves here. There are beginners' courses where you can learn the basic principles of this fascinating sport. Under the guidance of acknowledged diving instructors you dive one or more times. Hire of equipment and such is included in the price. For experienced divers there are special dive trips. Below a survey of the 'dive packages' the various diving operations on the island have to offer.

Aquaventure Dive Center
P.O. Box 88, Bonaire NA
tel. 8290, telex: 1926 HAMCO
This diving operation is located in Cap'n Don's Habitat and is the only five stars PADI diving operation on the island. Here they have both for the beginning and for the experienced diver diving courses and trips. You can also rent here all sorts of equipment you need for diving. Use of the equipment is included in the price of the courses. Furthermore they have an E-6 processor, so that underwater slides made, can be developed the very same day. Some price indications:
Courses:
PADI Open Water Course (for beginners): $ 290.-; Advanced Open Water Course: $ 160.-; Rescue Diver: $ 200.-; Divemaster: $ 350.-; Assistant Instructor: $ 200.-; Night Diver: $ 80.-; Deep Diver: $ 80.-; Underwater Photog-

raphy: $ 160.-; Wreck Diver: $ 80.-; Research Diver: $ 100.-; Search & Recovery Diver: $ 100.-.
Dive-packages and trips:
six days unlimited coast and boat diving: $ 215.-; six days unlimited coast diving: $ 75.-; six days with one boat dive and unlimited coast diving: $ 165.-, one guided dive: $ 33.-, unlimited number of guided dives per day: $ 44.-.

Bonaire Scuba Center
P.O. Box 106, Bonaire NA
tel. 8978, telex: 1291 HOBON
This diving operation is located near the Bonaire Beach Hotel. Here as well there are diving courses and trips for both beginning and experienced divers and it is possible to hire all diving equipment. Of course the use of the equipment is included in the price of the courses.
Price indications:
Courses:
Scuba Resort Course (one day instruction and one dive from the coast): $ 80.-; Scuba Certification Course (six days Open Water certification): $ 275.-;
Dive packages and trips:
Six days with each day one diving trip: $ 160.-; Six days with each day two dives: $ 220.-; one dive trip $ 33.- per day and in case of more than six times: $ 27.- per day. Two dive trips per day $ 44.- per day and in case of more than six days: $ 37.- per day (these dive trips include unlimited air, apparatus and weight belt).

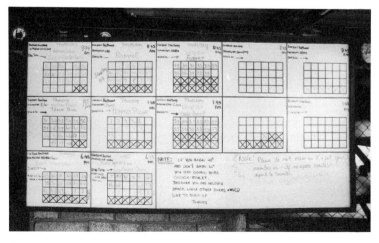

The planning board of the Bonaire Scuba Center

Buddy's Watersports

P.O.Box 231, Bonaire NA
tel. 8647 or 8065, telex: 1200 INPO
This dive operation is part of Buddy's Dive Resort. Here as well dive courses for advanced and beginning divers are organised. Furthermore you can hire all diving equipment here. Below some price indications:
Courses:
PADI Resort Course (for beginners): $ 80.- per person, in case of two or three persons: $ 60.- per person and in case of a group of four persons: $ 50.- per person; PADI Open Water Course (five days with five dives): $ 200.- (in case of two persons); PADI Advanced Open Water course (3 days, five dives, excluding equipment): $100.- per person.
Dive packages and trips:
A week unlimited diving (including apparatus, backpack, air, weight belt): $ 80.-; a week unlimited diving with a reef trip per day: $ 150.-; a week unlimited diving with two reef trips per day: $ 195.-. Five days unlimited diving: $ 60.-; five days unlimited diving with one reef trip per day: $ 100.-; one dive guided by an instructor: $ 18.-.

Carib Inn Dive Shop

P.O. Box 68, Bonaire NA
tel. 8819
NAUI and PADI dive facility, located near Bruce Bowker's Carib Inn. Here you can rent all diving equipment from flippers to backpack, and beginners' courses and reef trips for advanced divers are organised. Some price indications:
Courses:
Resort Course (two days instruction with three dives, complete with instructor and equipment): $ 125.-; Certification Course (NAUI or PADI beginners' course including instruction, equipment, etc.): $ 295.-; Advanced & Specialty Courses: $ 150.-.
Dive packages and trips:
Six days unlimited diving (with min. 12 boat dives including air, apparatus, weight belt): $ 199.-; Six days diving (six boat dives including air, apparatus, weight belt): $ 138.-; Unlimited coast diving (six days including apparatus, air, weight belt): $ 72.-; one boat dive: $ 11.-.

Dee Scarr's 'Touch the Sea'

P.O. Box 369, Bonaire NA
tel. 8529
Dee Scarr have its own program for divers who are inter-

ested in a personal approach. Divers already having the PADI certificate can acquire a special brevet 'Touch the Sea'. Dee Scarr has special underwater photography sessions in its package. This small, but very personal diving operation is open to guests of every hotel. Some price indications: One dive: $ 45.-; PADI Touch the Sea Certification (three dives): $ 135.- and furthermore there are possibilities for individually attuned arrangements.

Peter Hughes Dive Bonaire Kralendijk,
Bonaire NA
tel. 8285
Well-established and excellently equipped diving operation in the Flamingo Beach Hotel with no less than two dive shops: dive shop 1 and dive shop 2. Both the beginning and the advanced divers come into their own in the best possible way. There are beginners' courses as well as specialization courses and a large number of dive packages and dive trips available. Also all necessary diving equipment can be rented here. Furthermore there is an excellent underwater photography shop, where you can hire underwater cameras with all accessories needed. Moreover you can hire underwater video apparatuses and if desired, a professional underwater photographer to make underwater photos of yourself and other divers. Our experiences with this dive operation were simply excellent. Some price indications:
Courses:
Scuba Resort Course (instruction with beach dive, complete with instructor and equipment): $ 65.-; Full Certification Course (beginners' course including instruction, equipment and four dives): $ 300.-; and furthermore various Advanced & Specialty Courses.
Dive packages and trips:
Six Dive (6 boat dives and 1 night dive including air, apparatus, weight belt): $ 170.-; Unlimited diving (including apparatus, air and boat trips): $ 250.-. A boat dive (including apparatus, air, weight belt, and such): $ 25.-; night dive (including apparatus, air, weight belt and such): $ 25; dive trip to Washington-Slagbaai National Park with two dives (including apparatus, air, weight belt, and such): $ 50.-.

The Dive Inn
Kaya C.E.B. Hellmund 27, Bonaire NA
tel. 8761
PADI diving operation located immediately next to the Flamingo Beach Hotel in Kralendijk. This diving operation too

has beginners' courses, certificate courses and special dive trips for advanced divers. Furthermore you can rent all necessary equipment here. Some price indications:
Courses:
Scuba Resort Course (instruction with a dive, complete with instructor and equipment): $ 50.- (extra dives, if any, $ 35.-); PADI Certification Course (six days' beginners' course including instruction, equipment and dives): $ 215.-.
Dive packages and trips:
Week packages: unlimited diving from the coast (including air, apparatus, weight belt): $ 100.-; six boat dives and unlimited air (including apparatus and boat trips): $ 135.-; eleven boat dives and unlimited air (including apparatus and boat trips): $ 170.-. A boat dive (excluding apparatus, air, weight belt, and such): $ 8.-; water taxi to Klein Bonaire with at least four persons (excluding apparatus, air, weight belt, and such): $ 8.- per person.

Sand Dollar Dive & Photo
P.O. Box 175, Bonaire NA
tel. 8738
PADI dive operation located near the recently built Sand Dollar Condominiums & Beach Club under the management of André Nahr. Here as well an extensive package of services is available, for instance the rent of equipment, (be-

The landing stage of Capitain Don's Habitat & Hamlet

ginners')courses, dive trips, etc. There is a complete photo shop where underwater photography equipment can be rented. With this diving operation our experiences were very favorable. Some price indications:
Courses:
Scuba Resort Course (instruction with two dives, complete with instructor and equipment): $ 80.- (extra dives, if desired: $ 30.-); PADI International Open Water Certification Course (five days' beginners' course including instruction, equipment and dives): $ 280.-. For advanced: PADI Advanced Open Water Certification Course (five dives, excluding equipment): $ 160.-; PADI Rescue Diver Certification Course (instruction and five exercises, excluding equipment): $ 200.-.
Dive packages and trips:
Six days unlimited diving from the coast (including air and apparatus): $ 90.-; six boat dives and unlimited air (including apparatus and boat trips): $ 160.-; unlimited diving (including apparatus, air and boat trips): $ 210.-. One boat dive (excluding apparatus, air, weight belt and such): $ 12.-.

MAJOR DIVE SITES

In 1979 the Bonaire Marine Park was founded with as main objective preserving and protecting the vulnerable coral reefs and fish in the waters around Bonaire. For this purpose the sea around Bonaire to a depth of 200 feet was made a protected area. Subsequently, many measures were taken to protect the fish and the coral reefs. Apart from a ban on spear fishing issued before (1971), and a ban on collecting or taking away coral (1975), a number of specific park-rules were introduced, for instance the ban on damaging coral (by sitting or standing on it) and on fishing with other implements than a rod or handline. Furthermore, it is not allowed to come to anchor in the coral (special anchor buoys were placed to be used), objects found stuck between the coral must not be torn loose, in certain reserves diving of snorkeling is not allowed, etc. The aim is to keep the coral reefs and fish in the best possible condition, so that people may enjoy them for years to come. Apart from this people see to it, by means of scientific research, that the increasing use of the reefs does not lead to overexploitation with all the associated drawbacks. When necessary, for instance, certain - very popular - dive spots may be closed temporarily, if necessary for one or more years, if this is considered to be essential for the mending of the corals. Thanks to this reef control and observation of the park rules Bonaire belongs to the most beautiful diving paradises of the world nowadays.

The profile of the coral reefs of Bonaire is to a large degree the same everywhere, although there are small differences of course. The reefs are built up of different zones and as you come deeper, the physical circumstances change greatly. Below 130 to160 feet the coral growth decreases strongly and if you go deeper than 260 feet, you will find hardly any coral growing. The most beautiful bits of reef are found to a depth of 60 to 100 feet. In general reef coral needs quite a lot of sunlight to be able to grow and to a depth of 100 feet there is generally speaking enough sunlight for the coral to come to full bloom. If you go beyond 100 feet, in general you sell yourself short, for you unnecessarily shorten the diving time and there is hardly anything of interest to be seen any more. The first 100 feet are simply magnificent. In the surf we find in particular encrusting-colonials, algae, sea urchins and brain corals. In the shallow water to 15 feet we often find more than magnificent colonies of elkhorn coral. The branches of this coral grow 2 to 4 inches per year on average. Furthermore, we find at these shallow places the flat, light brown stinging coral. Take care you do not touch this coral, it can be compared to stinging-nettles, because touching it results in a burning

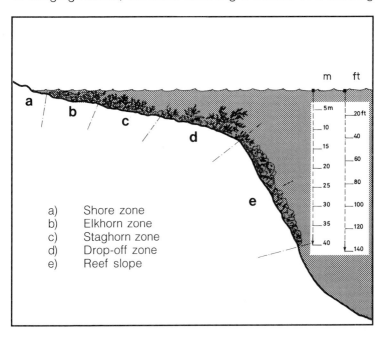

a) Shore zone
b) Elkhorn zone
c) Staghorn zone
d) Drop-off zone
e) Reef slope

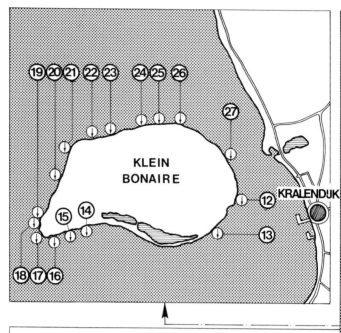

DIVE SITES:

1. Lighthouse (Willemstoren)
2. Red Slave (Oranje Pan, Pietiké, Leiké)
3. Pink Beach (White Pan, Cabajé)
4. Salt City (The Invisibles, Saliña Abou)
5. Alice in Wonderland
6. Angel City
7. The Lake
8. Punt Vierkant
9. Windsock Steep
10. Calabas Reef
11. Town Pier
12. Just-a-nice-dive (Kanal)
13. Nearest Point (Piedra Kolet)
14. South Bay
15. Hands Off
16. Forest
17. South-west Corner
18. Twixt
19. Valerie's Hill
20. Mi Dushi (Johanna's Revenge)
21. Carl's Hill (Punta P'Abou)

22. Jerry's Jam (Ebo's Special)
23. Leonora's Reef
24. Knife (Korontin)
25. Sampler
26. No Name (Playita)
27. Ebo's Reef
28. Something Special (Playa P'Abou)
29. Front Porch
30. La Machaca
31. Cliff
32. Small Wall
33. Petries Pillar
34. Oil Slick Leap
35. 1000 Steps (Piedra Haltu)
36. Ol' Blue
37. Rappel
38. La Dania's Leap
39. Karpata
40. Nukove (Doblet)
41. Boca Slagbaai
42. Playa Funchi
43. Playa Bengé
44. Boca Bartól

BONAIRE o MARINE PARK

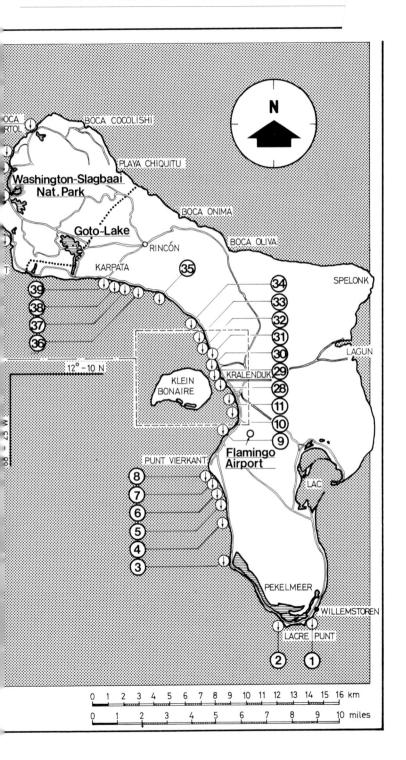

itching. If you go a bit deeper still, you often come to a plateau, consisting of white sand with relatively little vegetation. This sandy plateau is caused by sand slowly gliding
back into sea under the influence of the breakers. Due to
this gliding and moving to-and-fro of the breakers, the sea
organism hardly gets the chance to settle. This relatively
bare zone, gorgonian bushes and occasional coral vegetation are for instance found there, gradually changes into
parts with a richer underwater flora. Yellow-colored coral
hills alternate with the vulnerable staghorn coral (mind
breaking, for coral is a living organism!). When you are
about 30 feet deep, the reef goes down with an angle varying from 30 to 90 degrees. This transition is called Drop-off.
Out of the plane you can clearly see these transitions, because at these places the light blue color turns dark. On
these walls you find the greatest coral riches. The walls are
for the greater part covered with coral that has often flattened. In order to be able to catch the sunlight which
comes from above and is of vital importance. Past the drop-
off zone against the slanting and sometimes steep wall, we
find plate coral like roof tiles against the wall, but also black
coral, star coral, tube and pipe sponges. Between 30 and
100 feet depth we find a large variety of coral and other
sea organism. It will be obvious that to a depth of 100 feet a
great many beautiful things are to be seen. The reef continues to a depth varying from 100 to 200 feet, and then
changes into a sand terrace, with subsequently a second
drop-off, continuing to a depth varying from 150 to 275
feet. Here you find hardly any coral growth of importance.
The zones mentioned above do not just vary in depth, but
also in width (reckoned from the coast). The width of the
terrace from the coast to the drop-off varies between 70
and 530 feet (on the west coast in the south of Bonaire -
diving places 2 up to and including 8 -, the west coast - diving places 17 up to and including 20 - and east coast - diving places 12 and 27 - of Klein Bonaire this terrace is relatively wide, whereas on the north side of Klein Bonaire -
diving places 21 up to and including 26 - and the southwest
coast - diving places 34, 36 up to and including 39 - of Bonaire this terrace is relatively small). The drop-off depth is
fairly constant (about 30 feet), except for the east coast of
Klein Bonaire, where the drop-off starts already at a depth
of 3 to 7 feet (diving places 12 and 27). Drop-offs at an angle of 90 degrees hardly occur, only at the diving places
Carl's Hill (21), Cliff (31), Small Wall (32, Rappel (37) and La
Dania's (38) we can say there is a steep wall. On some
places - especially where the reef has a not too deep end

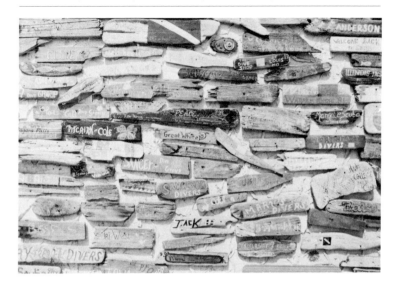

Many divers use wreckage to make a memorial

(less than 100 feet) - a second reef has come about, separated from the other by a sand canal (diving places 4 up to
and including 8). On some places you find giant, protruding
coral parts along the reef. Especially at the diving spots
Forest (16), Ebo's Reef (27), La Dania's (38), Karpata (39)
and Wayaka (41) you can find this kind of extreme coral
vegetation.
When diving for the first time on Bonaire, always consult an
experienced diver who knows the local situation or engage
a local dive instructor who knows the diving place well. Diving is a fascinating hobby, but you should never lose sight
of your personal safety. In the Bonaire Marine Park in total
44 diving places have been mapped by the stinapa. Below,
a short description of these places. The numbers corre-
spond with the numbers on the map. Some of the diving
places described below, can be reached from the coast,
others only by boat. At these latter diving places special
buoys have been placed so that the coral is not damaged
by anchors being cast. The diving places selected are
nearly all located on the west coast of Bonaire and around
Klein Bonaire. Due to the influence of the northeast tradewind the sea on the north and east side is too wild for safe
diving almost throughout the year. It is recommendable to
restrict oneself to the dive sites mentioned below. Briefly,
some information per dive site is given in order to make diving even more pleasant. For more detailed information I re-

fer to the Guide to the Bonaire Marine Park (Stinapa documentation series no. 11), an excellent diving guide. The information below has been taken from this guide (thanks to the Stinapa Bonaire for their kind permission). The diving operations mentioned before all organise dive trips to the dive sites mentioned below. So on the basis of the information you can judge for yourself what diving place looks the most attractive to you.

Park rules Bonaire Marine Park

1. Respect the marine environment and engage in no activities that may damage it (do not sit or step on corals - they are living animals! -, control your movements and your buoyancy).
2. The marine life is completely protected; there is no collecting (except for fishing with handlines or fishing rods and handcatching of non egg-bearing Spiny Lobster above 10 inches total length).
3. Spearguns and off course, spearfishing, are not allowed.
4. Anchors wreck coral and anchoring is not allowed in the coral (Except for emergency anchoring and anchoring by boats of less than 12 ft using a stone as anchor); between shore and the drop-off in the Town harbor area is an extensive sand-bottomed bay where anchoring is permitted.5. Artifacts cemented into the reef substratum may not be taken.
6. Fast boats are not allowed in Lac; their propellers whirl up silt and damage the seagrass beds.
7. Do not dive or snorkel in the marine reserves (the buoyed areas in between Karpata and Goto Lake and in between Playa Frans and Boca Slagbaai).
8. The mooring system is a public service; handle the moorings with care and remember that they are designed in such a way that, in order to be safely anchored, you must pay out extra line when tying to a mooring.

1. Lighthouse (Willemstoren)

This is a shore dive and only suited for experienced divers, because a good swimming ability is required to swim through the strong surf. You have to swim quite a distance through the surf, because the drop-off is at approximately 300 feet offshore at a depth of 33 to 40 feet. On the shallow terrace we find to a depth of 7 feet many flat rocks, some algae and Knobby Brain Coral. Gradually gorgonians, especially the Common Sea Fan, and Smooth Starlet Coral, Smooth Brain Coral and Knobby Brain Coral become more abundant. From about 10 feet the terrace is densely covered with gorgonians, stony corals and the brown alga Sargassum. From about 13 feet you will see some Elkhorn Coral and a few colonies Staghorn Coral. Between 23 and 50 feet, the drop-off zone, the coral and gorgonian growth is most lush: Sea Plumes, False plexaura, Common Sea Fans, Leaf Coral, Giant Brain Coral, Mountainous Star Coral, Smooth Starlet Coral, and Yellow Pencil Coral. Below 50 feet algae, small gorgonians and sponges dominate (especially (Deepwater Gorgonians and Tub Sponges). At 130 feet begins a deep sand terrace with numerous gorgonians and sponges. The recommended maximum diving depth is 50 to 60 feet. Concerning fish life, here you will see above the drop-off many grazing Parrotfish and Surgeonfish. Down to about 50 feet you will see Mahogany Snappers, Schoolmasters, Bluestriped Grunts, Coneys, Yellow Goatfish and an occasional Queen Triggerfish, Barracuda or a Spotted Moray Eel. Black Durgons are common in the drop-off zone and along the reef slope you see many Blue Chromis and several small Groupers (Coney, Graysby), large Tiger Groupers, some Nassau Groupers and an occasional big snapper. Snorkeling value is limited, unless the sea is calm.

2. Red Slave (Orange Pan, Pietiké, Leiké)
This is a shore dive and only suited for the more experienced divers. The drop-off is 300 feet offshore at a depth varying from 20 (north of the slave huts) to 40 feet (south of the slave huts). Coral cover is not high here, but this dive site is interesting because in 1829 the HMS Barham ran aground here and remains of this ship, such as anchors, ballast stones and other archaeological artifacts, are scattered over the bottom here. Along the entire south reef slope Gorgonians (Nodding Plexaurella and Deepwater Gorgonian) are abundant and a variety of sponges is found here. Black Corals are also present, but not as beautiful as on other dive sites. The most spectacular part,however, is the large number of big fish, such as Tiger Groupers, Yellowfin Groupers (approximately 4 ft), Grey Snappers, Black Margates, Midnight Parrotfish and a Southern Stingrays and an occasional Hawksbill Turtle. Yellowtail Snappers are also abundant. To the north (right, facing the sea) you will find an increasing number of deeply cut sand valleys. The reef on this north-side is less attractive. Gorgonians and sponges are initially abundant and coral cover is fairly high

on the buttresses, but the reef slope becomes progressively less attractive as you head north. The maximum diving depth for these reefs is 90 feet. Limited snorkeling value.

3. Pink Beach (White Pan, Cabajé)
This is a boat or shore dive for divers of all levels. The drop-off is 400 feet offshore at a depth of 33 feet. The shallow terrace is wide, gently sloping and all sand down to a depth of 13 feet. Staghorn Coral stretches all the way from 13 feet to about 30 feet. The reef slope has lush gorgonian growth and colorful sponges. At 90 feet begins a sand terrace with Garden Eels. To the South the shallow terrace is nearly all sand with occasionally some patches of Staghorn Coral. To the north there is around the drop-off zone a dense gorgonian forest and the remnants of three towers of Mountainous Star Coral. Fish life is abundant: Sergeant Majors, Royal Grammas, Black Margates, an Octopus, a Rock Hind, schools of Goatfish, Mahogany Snappers, Porgies, Yellowmouth Groupers, Tiger Groupers, Spotted Moray Eels and many more. Occasionally a Barracuda of 5 feet length may be seen. The recommended maximum diving depth is 90 feet. Fair snorkeling value.

4. Salt City (The Invisibles, Saliña Abou)
This site is situated at the southern end of the Alice in Wonderland (no. 5) double reef complex. It is a boat or shore dive and the drop-off is at 460 feet off the coast at a depth of 33 feet. This dive site is suited for divers of all levels. The shallow terrace is fairly wide and the bottom right offshore consists of hard rock with scattered Elkhorn Coral, Mustard Hill Coral, Fire Corals and some Gorgonians. Somewhat deeper (20 feet) you will find Staghorn Coral alternated with patches of sand. From 20 feet down towards the drop-off there is a mixture of Gorgonians with Staghorn Coral and Gorgonians with Mountainous Star Coral. From the shore entry point a wide sand patch is clearly visible. This wide sand path tapers to the drop-off and flows like a river down the reef slope into the sand terrace at 70-80 feet. This is the beginning of the double reef with on the other side a small coral 'island' at 60 feet. The reef slope does not have a high coral cover, but lush gorgonian growth. The slope is short and the sand plateau (with lots of Garden Eels and Sand Tilefish) is nowhere deeper than 100 feet. If you go northward and follow the sand channel you will pass various 'coral islands' sometimes as high as 30 feet. These 'islands' are extremely pretty, have lush coral growth and abundant sponges. Fish life on and over these 'coral is-

lands' is sensational. There are many Hose-eye Jacks, Tiger Groupers, Yellowmouth Groupers,Graysbys, Nassau Groupers, Yellowfin Groupers, Schoolmasters and Mahogany Snappers. The recommended maximum diving depth is 80 feet. Limited snorkeling value.

5. Alice in Wonderland

This site is part of the double reef complex that extends from Punt Vierkant (no. 8) to about halfway to the condensers south of the salt loading pier. It is a boat or shore dive and the drop-off is at 330 feet offshore at a depth of 23-30 feet. This dive site is suited for divers of all levels. The two reefs are separated by a sand channel of about 120 feet wide. On the shallow terrace you will see a lot of Staghorn Coral. Also small heads of Smooth Starlet Coral, Brain Coral and Mountainous Star Coral. The coral cover on the reef slope is fairly low, but the upper slope is lush with all types of corals and rather abundant Gorgonians. The reef slope goes down gently to the sand channel at a depth of 90 feet. After crossing the sand channel, the second reef will become visible. This second reef is richly grown with a large variety of coral sorts (including Giant Brain Coral, Mountainous Star Coral, Leaf Coral, Fungus Coral, Flower Coral and Cavernous Star Coral). On this second reef you will see many Yellowmouth Groupers and Tiger Groupers. The recommended maximum diving depth is 90 feet. Do not let yourself be tempted to descend along the second reef, for then you come much too deep. Limited snorkeling value.

6. Angel City

This dive site is very popular and part of the Alice in Wonderland double reef complex. It is a boat or shore dive and the drop-off is at 270 feet offshore at a depth of 30-33 feet. This dive site is suited for divers of all levels. On the gentle reef slope you will see a lot of Gorgonians and big boulders of Mountainous Star Coral. At a depth of 60 feet you will reach a sand channel, separating the first reef from the second. The face of the second reef is at 40 to 50 feet. If you swim south (keep the sand channel to your left) you will see how the second reef almost merges with the slope of the first reef. On this spot you can see magnificent boulders and temple-like structures of Mountainous Star Coral. The second reef reaches its most shallow point (30 ft) here. This is the place to be. Here you will see numerous fish, for instance Black Margates, Grey Snappers, Mahogany Snappers, a great many Sergeant Majors and off course Yellowtail Snappers. Furthermore you can see here many Coneys,

Graysbys, Parrotfish, Blue Tangs, Chromis and Creole Wrasses. This dive site is very popular for still another reason: on the 12th of September 1984 the freighter Hilma Hooker was sunk here (this ship had been confiscated after drugs had been found aboard), and this wreck is located on a sand-bank at about 90 feet depth. Starboard is at 90 feet and port at about 60 feet. This wreck is getting increasingly interesting. The recommended maximum diving depth here is 60 feet. Limited snorkeling value.

7. The Lake
This dive site is also part of the Alice in Wonderland double-reef complex. This is a boat or shore dive and the drop-off is at 330 feet offshore at a depth of about 30 feet. This dive site is suited for divers of all levels. The shallow terrace is covered with Staghorn Coral and some Yellow Pencil Coral. The second reef is separated by a narrow sand channel of 30 feet from the first reef. The upper reef slope has lush Gorgonians growth. From the lower edge of the first reef slope at 70 feet the second reef is clearly visible. Straight down from the mooring is a 'bridge' of coral heads connecting both reefs. The top of this second reef is at 60 feet under water. The many large 'towers' of 'temples' of Mountainous Star Coral create considerable relief. The most common coral species are Giant Brain Coral, Mountainous Star Coral, Flower Coral and Fungus Coral. Few Gorgonians and Black Corals occur. Bridges connect the two reefs in several places as you head south. Fish life includes Yellowtail Snappers, Yellowmouth Groupers, Graysbys, Coneys, Rock Hinds, Red Hinds, Nassau Groupers, Black Margates, Schoolmasters and Spotted Moray Eels. The recommended maximum diving depth is 70 feet. Limited snorkeling value.

8. Punt Vierkant
This site is situated at the northern end of the Alice in Wonderland double reef complex. This is a boat or shore dive and the drop-off is at 330 feet offshore at a depth of about 30 to 40 feet. This dive site is suited for divers of all levels. From the mooring down to the drop-off there is a lot of Gorgonians, Staghorn Coral and Mountainous Coral to be seen. On the reef slope Gorgonians and Sponges are abundant. From the lower edge of the reef slope at 90 feet where the sand channel begins the second reef is visible. Coral cover on the second reef is not so high, but Gorgonians and Sponges are abundant. Towards the south the reef moves up to 60 feet and the sand channel narrows. Coral cover becomes higher and at two spots we see a 'coral

bridge'. The second one is at 70 feet depth and has a diameter of 13 feet. A spectacular sight and very nice for underwater photos. Fish life on the second reef includes Jacks, Schoolmasters, Yellowmouth Groupers, Nassau Groupers and Yellowtail Snappers. The sand channel is the habitat of the Garden Eel, Palometa and Southern Stingray. The recommended maximum diving depth is 90 feet. Limited snorkeling value.

9. Windsock Steep
This is a boat or shore dive and the drop-off is at 200 feet offshore at a depth of about 20-27 feet. This dive site is suited for divers of all levels. Especially for beginners this place is ideal. The shallow terrace has some patches of Elkhorn Coral, Fire Coral and Staghorn Coral, which, however, was severely damaged during a storm in November 1984. The drop-off zone is sandy, but the reef slope is typical and attractive decorated with Gorgonians and Sponges. Fish life includes quite a variety of fish: Ocean Triggerfishes, Tiger Groupers, Yellowmouth Groupers, Sergeant Majors, Schoolmasters, Rock Hinds, Queen Angelfish, French Angelfish (magnificent!), Bluestriped Grunts, Mahogany Snappers, etc. You can also frequently find Barracudasand Moray Eels here. The recommended maximum diving depth is 70 feet. Limited snorkeling value.

10. Calabas Reef
This is Bonaire's most frequently dived site according to the dive statistics. That is because it is located opposite the Flamingo Beach Hotel and all divers staying at the hotel and/or diving with Dive Bonaire will make their 'warm-up dive' here. This is a shore dive and suited for divers of all levels. The drop-off is at 200 feet offshore at a depth of 33 to 40 feet. The shallow terrace consists of a sand area towards the drop-off, with just before it some Gorgonians and some Mountainous Star Coral. The reef slope straight down from the Dive Bonaire dock is quite attractive and beautifully overgrown with a large variety of corals (Giant Brain Coral, Cavernous Star Coral) and many sponges. To the north the slope becomes less attractive - due to frequent anchoring by yachts -, but north of the Calabas Restaurant pier at 60 feet depth is the wreck of an aluminum boat, sunk by Captain Don Stewart. There are Christmas Tree Worms, Sponges and Fire Coral growing on the hull. The northernmost of the moorings in front of the hotel is a beautifully overgrown 10 feet long, old anchor at 27 feet depth. The pier of the Calabas Restaurant grows Encrusting Stinging Coral and

Orange Tube Coral. This is a good snorkeling spot. Fish life is abundant in the shallow area: Mullets, Goatfish, French Angelfish, Parrotfish, Surgeonfish, Spanish Hogfish, Bicolor Damselfish and of course Yellowtail Snappers). The recommended maximum diving depth is 70 feet.

11. Town Pier

A popular and rather unusual dive site. It is a shore dive and for safety reasons the diving here is subject to permission from the harbormaster. The Town Pier refers to the 'old pier', located in between the customs office and the fish market. The main attraction of diving here is the rich invertebrate life on the pillars of the pier and the abundance of fish sheltering underneath or close to the pier. It is the spot for close-up and macrophotography. The pillars are covered with corals (notably Butterprint Brain Coral), Purple Tube Sponges, Do-not-touch-me Sponges, Orange Tube Corals, Encrusting Sponges in orange, green and purple, bright Yellow Sponges, Christmas Tree Worms and lots of Arrow Crabs. Especially at night when the corals become active, it is a magnificent and beautiful sight. Orange, green, purple, brown ..... you can see here the most beautiful coral colours under this pier at only a few feet depth. Fish life under the pier is also remarkably: Sergeant Majors, Redlip Blennies, Redspotted Hawkfish, Smallmouth Grunts, juvenile French Grunts and Needlefish. In addition you will see Mahogany Snappers, Queen Angelfish, French Angelfish, Damselfish, Smooth Trunkfish, Honeycomb Cowfish, Trumpetfish, Blue Tangs, Ocean Surgeons, Doctorfish, Barracudas and on the sand-bottom Yellowfin Mojarras and Yellow Goatfish. You may also see the rare Frogfish. In the late afternoon you can take magnificent underwater photos here. The recommended maximum diving depth is 30 feet and this siteoffers good snorkeling value.

12. Just-a-nice-dive (Kanal)

This dive site is located on the east coast of Klein Bonaire. It is a boat dive and suited for divers of all levels. The dropoff at this site is very shallow (3 - 7 feet). As suggested by the name, diving here is nice but not special. because of the location in the lee of Kralendijk harbor, this area is littered with bottles that drifted across from town to Klein Bonaire and eventually sank on the reef. Some of the bottles are over a hundred years old! On the shallow terrace you will see scattered Elkhorn Coral, patches of Staghorn Coral, small heads of Brain Coral and Gorgonians. The reef slope is a system of buttresses and valleys. Yellow Pencil Coral,

Diver at Town Pier

Slave huts near the Salt Lake

Parrot fish

Spotted drum fish

Green morays

Frog fish

Club Finger Coral, Leaf Coral and to a lesser degree Mountainous Star Coral and Black Coral are common here. Large Orange Sponges) are quite abundant. The buttresses show considerable relief. Fish life includes numerous Parrotfishes and Blue Tangs. Abundant fish life is seen in the drop-off zone and upper reef slope: Yellowtail Snappers, some big Tiger groupers, White-spotted Filefish, Ocean Triggerfish, Yellow Goatfish, Sergeant Majors, Mahogany Snappers and Bermuda Chubs. The recommended maximum diving depth is 80 feet. Fair snorkeling value.

13. Nearest Point (Piedra Kolet)
This dive site is about the nearest point of Klein Bonaire seen from the Flamingo Beach Hotel. It is a boat dive and suited for divers of all levels. The drop-off starts at 20 to 30 feet. The shallow terrace from 10 feet up is rather barren of coral, sandy with staghorn rubble and some Gorgonians. De drop-off zone is sandy, but otherwise characterized by the presence of Gorgonians, Mountainous Star Coral, Smooth Starlet Coral and Giant Brain Coral. On the upper reef slope you will see much Flower Coral, patches of Yellow Pencil Coraland some big Orange Sponges and Purple Tube Sponges. On the lower reef slope you will see Mountainous Star Coral, Sheet Coral and some good-sized Black Coral. At about 100 and 130 feet depth some extensive untouched areas of Sheet Coral and Scroll Coral can been found. Fish life consists of Yellowtail Snapper, Groupers and some Spotted Moray Eels. The silvery Palometa fish can be found on the upper reef slope and the shallow terrace. They can be fed by hand (bits of bread or cheese). The recommended maximum diving depth is 90 feet. Limited snorkeling value.

14. South Bay
This dive site is located on the exposed side of Klein Bonaire and therefore a light to moderate chop is to be expected. This is also a boat dive and suited for divers of all levels, provided the sea is not too rough. The drop-off starts at 33-40 feet. The shallow terrace is divided in two by a 'step' at about 13 feet. The upper part is a hardrock plateau, covered with Gorgonians and small heads of Smooth Starlet Coral and Brain Corals. The lower terrace is characterized by lush Gorgonians and scattered small heads of Mountainous Star Coral. On the upper reef slope the Club-Finger Coral, Yellow Pencil Coral and Flower Coral are quite common. Gorgonians are rather abundant and you will also find Black Corals. The lower reef slope is covered exten-

sively with Sheet Corals. Towards the west (right) are some very pronounced buttresses and valleys and a couple of small vertical walls. The first wall is the home of the famous Spotted Moray Eel, called Benedict Arnold. Expect to see furthermore some big Tiger Groupers, Yellowtail Snappers, Horse-eye Jacks and big Schoolmasters here. The recommended maximum diving depth is 90 feet. This dive site offers good snorkeling value when the sea is calm.

15. Hands Off

Like all dive sites around Klein Bonaire, this is also a boat dive. This site is only accessible for experienced divers (within the scope of a research to find out in how far not-experienced divers cause more damage to the reef than experienced divers, this site is closed for unexperienced divers and divers with underwater cameras). The drop-off starts at 27 feet. The shallow terrace is sandy with some Gorgonians and small heads of Mountainous Star Coral. The upper terrace is covered with staghorn rubble and some Staghorn Coral, Pinktipped Anemones and many Gorgonians. The drop-off zone is narrow with numerous Gorgonians. The reef slope, down to 70 feet, is covered with big heads of Mountainous Star Coral, Cavernous Star Coral, Giant Brain Coral, a lot of Flower Coral, Yellow Pencil Coral and a large variety of sponges. Expect here some Big Tiger Groupers, Yellowmouth Groupers and Rock Hinds. At the drop-off zone you will see many Black Durgons and more shallow Bermuda Chubs and big Parrotfishes like the Midnight and Rainbow Parrotfish. The recommended maximum diving depth is 90 feet. Limited snorkeling value.

16. Forest

This dive site got its name from the presence of large quantities of Black Coral ('A Black Coral forest'). It is a boat dive and not suited for novice divers. The drop-off is at 27 feet. The shallow terrace is divided in an upper and a lower terrace with a 'step' at 13 feet. The upper terrace is hard rock covered with sand and many loose coral fragments. On the lower terrace Gorgonians are quite abundant. Look around the Gorgonians for hidden tiny White-spotted Filefishes. The drop-off zone is covered with lush Mountainous Star Coral and Gorgonians. On the upper reef slope Mountainous Star Coral is dominant, in addition Flower Coral, Giant Brain Coral, patches of Yellow Pencil Coral and Club Finger Coral are abundant. Sponges (especially the Orange Sponge) are quite common. On the lower reef slope, below 80 feet, nice Sheet Corals occur. Straight down from the mooring is a near-vertical buttress, going down to 70 feet only, with two caves, one at 90 feet, the other at 70 feet on the Hands-off side of the buttress. Most Black Coral grows on the crest and the eastern side of the buttress. Fish life includes big Tiger Groupers, Schoolmasters, Mahogany Snappers, Blues-striped Grunts, Horse-eye Jacks, Queen Angelfish, French Angelfish and in thedrop-off zone Black Durgons. Also a lot of Yellowtail Snappers are around. A friendly Spotted Moray Eel lives near the cave at 90 feet. The recommended diving depth is 90 feet. Good snorkeling value when the sea is calm.

17. South West Corner

This dive site at the south-western tip of Klein Bonaire is very popular. That is no surprise, because the underwater world here is very colorful. It is a boat dive and suited for divers of all levels. The drop-off is at 30 feet. The shallow terrace is very nice. Between 23 and 13 feet is a mix of Staghorn Coral and Mountainous Star Coral and abundant Gorgonians. From 13 feet up there are less Gorgonians but the Staghorn Coral continues, along with some patches of Elkhorn Coral and isolated Fire Coral and Mountainous Star Coral. Among the Staghorn Coral you can find many Pink-tipped Anemones and the Common Lettuce Slug.
In the drop-off zone large numbers of Gorgonians occur. Seaward of the mooring on the drop-off at about 33 feet is a Purple Tube Sponge with more than 40 individual tubes. The reef slope has a great variety of invertebrates. Gorgonians and Black Corals are well-represented. A variety of Sponges and coral sorts (Mountainous Star Coral, Giant Brain Coral, Black Coral) adds to the overall colorful aspect of the reef slope. A bit south-east of the mooring, at 73 feet is a nice old anchor with four flukes. Fish life includes Sergeant Majors, Yellowmouth Groupers, White-spotted Filefish, Schoolmasters and Yellowtail Snappers. Moreover large Tiger Groupers, an occasional Oceanfish, Triggerfish and various Parrotfish can be seen here. The recommended maximum diving depth is 80 feet. Limited snorkeling value.

18. Twixt

This is a boat dive and suited for divers of all levels. The drop-off is at 40 feet. The shallow terrace is wide and an extensive field of Staghorn Coral stretches from 27 feet to about 10 feet. Interspersed with the Staghorn Coral are Fire Corals, Gorgonians, heads of Giant Brain Coral, Mountainous Star Coral, Brain Corals and Yellow Pencil Coral.

From 10 feet to the surface you will find the usual Elkhorn Coral plus patches of Leafy Stinging Coral and Club Finger Coral. The drop-off zone is rather barren, but Gorgonians are present all along. The reef slope shows no distinct zonation, although some Sheet Coral and Scroll Coral is typical for the lover slope. Black Coral, Gorgonians and Sponges are plentiful. Fish life includes large schools of Chromis, Creole Wrasses and farther out of the reef at depths from about 20 to 70 feet Horse-eye Jacks. Along the reef slope large Tiger groupers and Yellowmouth Groupers are common. The shallow terrace is also very lush with life: Trumpetfish, Spanish Hogfish, Coneys, Goldentail Morays and Spotted Moray Eels. The recommended maximum diving depth is 80 feet. Good snorkeling value.

19. Valerie's Hill

This site was named after Captain Don Stewart's wife Valerie. Itis similar to Twixt with lots of Sponges and Black Coral. It is a boat dive and suited for divers of all levels. The drop-off is at 30 feet. The shallow terrace has till 10 feet depth much Elkhorn Coral and from 23 to 10 feet there is a dense field of Staghorn Coral. From 33 to 23 feet the shallow terrace is rather barren with scattered Gorgonians. The drop-off zone has low coral cover. On the upper reef slope the Mountainous Star Coral forms large structures. Sponges are abundant along the reef slope, especially Purple Tube Sponges and Orange Sponges. Black Coral is also abundant here, but Gorgonians are not, apart from the Encrusting Gorgonian. The lower reef slope has Sheet Corals and Scroll Corals. On this side of Klein Bonaire you can see many large Groupers, as well as Coneys and Graysbys. Moreover you can attract here often less common fish, such as a Scrawled Filefish or the Grey Parrotfish. The recommended maximum diving depth is 90 feet. Good snorkeling value.

20. Mi Dushi (Johanna's Revenge)

The mooring on this site was originally placed for the Mi Dushi, a boat that ran one-day charter trips with tourists. This dive site is named after this boat. There is a small beach here with easy entrance to the sea, so it is boat dive as well as a shore dive. It is suited for divers of all levels. The drop-off is at 33 to 40 feet. The shallow terrace is wide and for the greater part covered with Staghorn Coral with in between Yellow Pencil Coral, Mountainous Star Coral, Mustard Hill Coral, Elliptical Star Coral and Fire Coral. Close to the shore is a zone with Elkhorn Coral. In the drop-off zone

Gorgonians (Dry Sea Plumes, Slimy Sea Plumes, False Plexaura, Sea Rod and Encrusting Gorgonian) are abundant, but coral cover is low. Along the reef slope to the southwest you will find well-developed buttresses and on the second one left of the mooring, at about 60 feet is the 'Wagon Wheel' sponge, a Purple Tube Sponge which has grown like a half wagon wheel with spokes. Sponges are abundant and varied. To the south-west you can find quite a lot of Black Coral. Fish life includes some big Tiger Groupers and Yellowmouth Groupers, furthermore Redspotted Hawkfish, Graysbys, Coneys, Rock Hinds and Red Hinds. Also a Seahorse is to be admired here. The recommended maximum diving depth is 90 feet. Fair snorkeling value.

21. Carl's Hill (Punta P'Abou)

This dive site has been named after the famous underwater photographer Carl Roessler. It is a boat dive and suited for divers off all levels. The drop-off is at 33 feet. This dive site is famous for its vertical wall just east of the mooring. The wall stretches form 33 to 67 feet. The shallow terrace straight up from the wall is more narrow than anywhere else on Klein Bonaire. On the terrace you will see close to the shore the usual Elkhorn Coral and deeper some Gorgonians, Fire Coral, Staghorn Coral and Brain Coral. On the upper part of the wall you will find lots of Cavernous Star Coral in colors from green to purple to red, and Butterprint Brain Coral. there is a variety of Sponges on the wall and the colors are exciting. Black Corals,especially Black Wire Coral are also present on the wall. The deepest part of the wall has some flat Sheet Corals. Fish life is impressive here. There are several resident Spotted Moray Eels and it is also possible to see here a very large (6 to 7 feet) Green Moray Eel swimming free. West of the mooring is no vertical wall, but a nice reef with at about 60 feet a large Purple Tube Sponge with in excess of 70 tubes! The recommended maximum diving depth is 70 feet. Limited snorkeling value.

22. Jerry's Jam (Ebo's Special)

This is a very popular dive site, originally named after Bonaire's first dive guide Hubert 'Ebo' Domacasse and later after underwater photographer Jerry Greenberg. It is a boat dive and one of the most popular dive sites of Bonaire. It is suited for divers of all levels. The shallow terrace is extremely narrow and the reef begins to slope right down from the barrier of Elkhorn Coral, without an actual drop-off. The upper reef slope has large Giant Brain Corals and towers of Mountainous Star Coral in all shapes. There are some subtle buttresses. The lower reef slope has the characteristic roof shingle formations of Sheet Corals and Mountainous Star Coral. There are two outstanding characteristics of the fish life: the first is that there are always a lot of fish; the second is the great variety of fish life: Groupers, Spanish Hogfish, Yellowtail Snappers, Scrawled Filefish, Trumpetfish, various Goatfish and Grunts. The recommended maximum diving depth is 90 feet. Very good snorkeling value. Underwater photographers must not miss Jerry's Jam/Ebo's Special!

23. Leonora's Reef

This dive site is located on the north side of Klein Bonaire. It is a boat dive and suited for divers of all levels. The drop-off is at 23 to 30 feet. The shallow terrace is narrow and generally covered extensively with Yellow Pencil Coral, Fire Corals and Mountainous Star Coral. Elkhorn Coral is found close to the shore. Just below the drop-off Mountainous Star Coral, Giant Brain Coral, Yellow Pencil Coral and Flower Coral are the most common species. There are also some very nice Pillar Coral formations near the mooring. The upper reef slope has a high percentage of coral and a high relief. Most abundant here are Flower Coral, Club Finger Coral and Yellow Pencil Coral. There are hardly any Sponges, Gorgonians or Black Coral. Fish life includes some big Tiger Groupers and Yellowmouth Groupers and sometimes the rare Yellowfin Grouper. Yellowtail Snappers are also common here. The recommended maximum diving depth is 80 feet. Good snorkeling value.

24. Knife (Korontin)

This a typically lush Bonairean dive site, with nice coral formations. It is a boat dive and suited for divers of all levels. The drop-off is at 20 to 33 feet. The shallow terrace is extremely pretty with Elkhorn Coral, large clumps of the fragile Yellow Pencil Coral, Mountainous Star Coral, Fire Coral, Staghorn Coral and Leaf Coral. The drop-off zone is rather barren of coralgrowth. Gorgonians are common here and you will see the Encrusting Stinging Coral, Yellow Pencil Coral, and Encrusting Gorgonians. The upper reef slope has some fairly big towers of Mountainous Star Coral. The reef has not much relief and there is no distinct zonation. Neither Gorgonians nor Black Corals are very abundant here. The fish life is very interesting. There are two French Angelfish that like to be fed (bits of banana or cheese, please) and also one or two Ocean Triggerfish are often seen here. A large number of Tiger Groupers seems to be characteristic for this area. Bermuda Chubs can be found near the mooring. The recommended maximum diving depth 80 feet. This site is extremely good for snorkeling.

25. Sampler

Characteristic for this dive site are a narrow shallow terrace and a shallow drop-off. It is a boat dive and suited for divers of all levels. The reef begins to slope down from 13 to 17 feet. The shallow terrace is a sandy plateau with scattered Brain Coral, Mustard Hill Coral and Mountainous Star Coral. Near the shore you will find Yellow Pencil Coral, Fire Corals and Elkhorn Coral. The upper reef slope has a lot of Mountainous Star Coral and furthermore Yellow Pencil Coral, Flower Coral and Fire Corals. The lower reef slope has some pretty roof shingle formations, made up of Sheet Corals and flattened Mountainous Star Coral. Fish life includes large Yellowmouth Groupers, Tiger Groupers and of course Yellowtail Snappers. An Ocean Triggerfish is not uncommon here. Sampler has some special residents: an adult Spanish Hogfish called 'Gladiator', a French Angelfish called 'D'Artagnan' (to be recognized by a tiny white spot in the very center of his left eye) and two Spotted Moray Eels, called 'Candide' and 'Flattail'. You can feed these fish by hand, but do not bring fish down for feeding. The eels could become dangerous. The recommended maximum diving depth is 80 feet. Good snorkeling value.

26. No Name (Playita)

This dive site is located along the only sizable, very popular beach at Klein Bonaire. It is a good spot for a picnic and also a good starting point for snorkeling trips. This site is suited for divers of all levels. The drop-off is 100 feet offshore at a depth of 20 feet. The shallow terrace is close to the mooring sandy. Near the shore Staghorn Coral is present. The drop-off zone is shallow, sandy with some small Brain Corals and Mountainous Star Corals; Flower Coral and Yellow Pencil Coral are abundant. The reef slope is very nice from 33 feet down and from 80 feet beautiful roof shingle formations are found. Black Coral is fairly abundant. To the west the reef slope shows a system of buttresses and valleys. The buttresses are covered with Fire Coral, Flower Coral and Yellow Pencil Coral. Fish life includes the rare Mullet and furthermore big Tiger Groupers, Yellowmouth Groupers, Schoolmasters and an occasional Yellowfin Grouper. The recommended maximum diving depth is 90 feet. Good snorkeling value.

27. Ebo's Reef

This dive site has the highest density of Black Corals of all Bonaire. It is a boat dive and suited for divers of all levels. The drop-off is very shallow (3 to 7 feet) and the shallow terrace is less than 7 feet deep. It is sandy, with lots of small Brain Corals, Mustard Hill Coral, some Elkhorn Coral and Staghorn Coral. The reef slope shows little zonation. The sand/rubble valleys are very unstable habitat where numerous Do-not-touch-me Sponges occur. On the upper part Yellow Pencil Coral is abundant and beautiful Deepwater Gorgonians can be seen more to the south. This site is especially famous for its beautiful Orange Sponges and the abundant presence of Black Coral, which can be found here as shallow as 20 feet. Fish life includes large numbers of Yellowtail Snappers and furthermore Mahogany Snappers, Tiger Groupers and an Ocean Triggerfish. North of the mooring a school of Goatfish can be found and one or two Spotted Scorpionfish can be found camouflaged along the buttress, which is also the home of a Coral Crab and two Spotted Moray Eels. The recommended maximum diving depth is 90 feet. Limited snorkeling value.

28. Something Special (Playa P'Abou)

This dive site is well-known for its colony of Garden Eels that lives on the sand terrace from 60 feet down. It is a boat dive and suited for divers of all levels. The drop-off is at 23 to 30 feet. The sand terrace begins at 50 feet south of the entrance of the Marina and slopes down to a depth of 100 feet and beyond. You have to approach the Garden Eels gently, otherwise the will retreat into their burrows. If you approach them gently, you can get as close a 7 feet. The reef slope has a lot of Sponges, especially the Purple Bleeding Sponges living in symbiosis with an Orange Colonial Anemone. Fish life includes a lot of Scorpionfish and Spotted Moray Eels, Creole Fish, Smallmouth Grunts and Mahogany Snappers. At the tip of the southern groin of the Marina Entrance you will see abundant Schoolmasters, Bluestriped Grunts, Sergeant Majors, Bermuda Chubs and Black Margates. The recommended maximum diving depth is 90 feet. Limited snorkeling value. For safety reasons we do not recommend crossing the entrance of the marina to the north-west.

29. Front Porch

This dive site is in front of the Bonaire Beach Hotel and a lot of guests will make their 'warm-up dive' here. It is a shore dive only and it is suited for divers of all levels. You enter from the pier of the Bonaire Scuba Center. There is a narrow sand flat, that begins to slope down already at 10 feet. The pier itself is quite interesting: with lots of Orange Tube Coral and abundant Sergeant Majors, Yellowtail Snappers, Redlip Blennies, juvenile French Grunts and often some large Barracudas. On the reef slope are many Purple Tube Sponges and among the living coral Cavernous Star Coral dominates. Swimming to the north (facing sea) you will find an old anchor at 23 feet depth, overgrown by all kinds of invertebrates. Fish life along the reef slope consists of Graysbys, Rock Hinds, Goatfish, Creole Fish, Sergeant Majors and plenty of Yellowtail Snappers. If you dive towards the Marina you will find a very gentle reef slope with an extensive field of Do-not-touch-me Sponges and further on Purple Sprawling Sponges and Pink-tipped Anemones. Do not expect a beautiful reef here. The recommended maximum diving depth is 80 feet. Limited snorkeling value.

30. La Machaca

This is the dive site where divers staying at Captain Don's Habitat & Hamlet will make take their 'warm-up dive'. It is a shore dive and you start from the dock of Captain Don's Habitat. It is suited for divers of all levels. The drop-off is 150 feet offshore at 20 to 33 feet. The shallow terrace has from 10 to 20 feet a field of Staghorn Coral. Also characteristic are small colonies of Mustard Hill Coral, Fire Corals, some Fused Staghorn Coral and near the shore lush Elkhorn Coral. At a depth of 20 feet the shallow terrace begins to slope down. At 33 feet lies a small wreck sunk there by captain Don. The reef slope begins at 33 feet and the lower edge is at 120 feet, where you can have look at the Garden Eels in the sand terrace. On the upper part of the reef slope Gorgonians are common. Also on the slope are Giant Brain Coral, Mountainous Star Coral and a beautiful colony of Pillar Coral. On the lower slope are nice roof shingle formations of Sheet and Scroll Coral. Fish life includes Sergeant Majors, Surgeonfish, Parrotfish, Yellow Goatfish, Trumpetfish, Spanish Hogfish, a Spotted Moray Eel, a Tiger Grouper and sometimes a 5 feet big Tarpon. The recommended maximum diving depth is 120 feet. Very good snorkeling value.

31. Cliff

This is a boat or shore dive and suited for divers of all levels. The drop-off is 120 feet offshore at 30 feet depth. You enter from the small beach through a with Club Finger Coral carpeted channel in the Elkhorn Coral and Fire Corals barrier. Watch out for the Sea Urchins as you pass through. Next you get a barren sand flat with some Fire Coral, Mustard Hill Coral, Brain Corals and coral rubble. The upper reef slope is a vertical wall from 30 feet down to 60 feet, which is covered with Cavernous Star Coral, Sheet Corals, Encrusting Gorgonians, Encrusting Sponges, Black Wire Coral and other small Black Corals. This wall is a grateful subject for underwater photography. Fish life at the shallow sand terrace includes Lizardfish, Peacock Flounder, Scorpionfish and sometimes a Yellowhead Jawfish. At the wall Royal Grammas and yellowtail Snapper are abundant. The recommended maximum diving depth is 60 feet. This whole area is excellent for snorkeling.

32. Small Wall

This is a shore or boat dive and suited for divers of all levels. The drop-off is 230 feet offshore at a depth varying from 23 to 33 feet. As the name suggests this site is characterized by the presence of a small wall. The shallow terrace has just off the shore a narrow encrusted barrier of Elkhorn Coral with Fire Corals and Encrusting Colonial Anemones. From 10 feet down to the beginning of the drop-off you will see a lot of Staghorn Coral with in between patches of Yellow Pencil Coral, some Brain Coralsand small heads of Mountainous Star Coral. The wall is located southeast of the mooring. It starts at 40 feet and goes down to about 67 feet. Gorgonians are abundant at the upper edge of the wall, and along the vertical slopes are various Sponges, Black Wire Coral, large flattened Sheet Coral, Fungus Coral and a great deal of Cavernous Star Coral. Fish life includes a pair of Scrawled Filefish, some Barracuda, various Snappers, Tiger Groupers and Tarpons. Near the drop-off zone Lizardfish and Peacock Flounders are present and on the shallow terrace Trumpetfish are plentiful. The recommended maximum diving depth is 90 feet. Limited snorkeling value.

33. Petries Pillar

This dive site was named after a colony of Pillar Coral that is located just north-west of the mooring. It towers some 4 feet above the reef face. It is a boat or shore dive and suited for divers of all levels. The drop-off is 300 feet off shore and starts at 33 to 40 feet depth. The shallow terrace has a barrier of Elkhorn Coral starting at about 10 feet and a fairly extensive zone of Elkhorn Coral between 20 and 27 feet. In between are Encrusting Colonial Anemones, Yellow Pencil Coral, Staghorn Coral, Pink-tipped Anemones, Fire Corals,

Brain Corals and Mountainous Star Coral. The drop-off zone is rather barren and on the upper reef slope are many Gorgonians. The lower reef slope has nice formations of Sheet Coral and Scroll Coral. Fish life: Some Barracuda, and Tiger Groupers and Yellowmouth Groupers are numerous. You can also see a Seahorse here. The recommended maximum diving depth is 90 feet. Fair snorkeling value.

34. Oil Slick Leap

This is a boat dive and suited for divers of all levels. The drop-off zone is at 33 feet depth. The shallow terrace is quite narrow at the mooring site. The upper part from 10 feet is a near vertical cliff covered with Orange Tube Coral, Leaf Coral, Fire Coral and Gorgonians. From 10 to 20 feet you will find a lot of Yellow Pencil Coral, Fire Corals, Brain Coral and Gorgonians. from 20 to 27 feet is a narrow zone with Staghorn Coral. The drop-off zone is characterized by many Gorgonians. The reef slope has little zonation, but from 100 feet down typical roof shingle structures of Mountainous Star Coral, Sheet Coral and Scroll Coral are found. The lower reef slope has abundant Gorgonians. Fish life includes Yellowtail Snappers, Tiger Groupers, Yellowmouth Groupers and a French Angelfish, Queen Angelfish, Scrawled Filefish, Whitespotted Filefish or a Barracuda. The recommended maximum diving depth is 100 feet. Limited snorkeling value.

35. 1000 Steps (Piedra Haltu)

This is a boat or shore dive (if you do not mind the steps!) and it is suited for divers of all levels. The drop-off is 200 feet offshore and begins at 33 feet depth. The shallow is sandy with Gorgonians, scattered Elkhorn Coral and a lot of broken Staghorn Coral. Near the drop-off zone are some big towers of MountainousStar Coral. They are nearly all cleaning stations serviced by juvenile Spanish hogfish and Bluehead Wrasses. Gorgonians are abundant in this zone. The upper reef slope is dominated by Mountainous Star Coral and the lower reef slope has abundant Sheet Coral and Scroll Coral. This site is a good place to watch the cleaning symbiosis. Fish life includes Sergeant Majors, various Parrotfish, Spanish Hogfish, Bluehead Wrasses, small Groupers and if you are very attentive, you may see the rare Shovelnosed Lobster here. The recommended maximum diving depth is 90 feet. Limited snorkeling value.

36. Ol' Blue

This is a shore dive only and it is suited for divers of all levels. The drop-off is 100 feet offshore at 30 feet depth. The first part of the shallow terrace is sandy, then some Mountainous Star Coral and Gorgonians appear, gradually changing into a mixed Mountainous Star Coral and Gorgonians community close to the drop-off. Just below the drop-off zone Yellow Pencil Coral is abundant and on the upper reef slope Mountainous Star Coral and Flower Coral are present. Sheet Coral and Scroll Coral are to be found on the lower reef slope. Fish life includes a lot of Mahogany Snappers, Yellowtail Snappers, Schoolmasters, Tiger Groupers, Yellowmouth Groupers and Black Durgons here. You may also see some Barracuda, a school of Horse-eye Jacks or the Scrawled Filefish. The recommended maximum diving depth is 90 feet. Limited snorkeling value, but if you do not mind snorkeling for 20 to 30 minutes then you must go to the east where close to the cliff at a depth of 20 feet three large and two smaller limestone blocks can be found, covered with Gorgonians, Sponges and a variety of corals. They are quite attractive.

37. Rappel

This is one of the most spectacular dive sites of Bonaire. It is a boat dive and suited for divers of all levels. The drop-off starts at 37 to 40 feet depth and is close to the mooring. The terrace is extremely narrow and the boat has to be moored very close to the shore which is a sheer cliff. This cliff continues underwater almost vertically down to a depth of 30 feet. The shallow terrace is covered with massive Mountainous Star Corals, Giant Brain Coral, Yellow Pencil Coral and some patches of Staghorn Coral. The cliff wall is covered with corals and Gorgonians. It is a colorful world with lot of Orange Tube Coral and many colored encrusting Sponges. The shallow terrace is covered with Mountainous Star Coral, Giant Brain Coral, Yellow Pencil Coral and occasional patches of Staghorn Coral. The upper reef slope has massive boulders of Mountainous Star Coral and large Giant Brain Corals. There are few Gorgonians and Black Corals and not many Sponges. The lower reef slope is densely covered with roof shingle formations of Sheet Coral and Scroll Corals. The lush coral growth provides homes for a variety of fish: Tiger Groupers, Yellowmouth Groupers, Yellowfin Groupers, Horse-eye Jacks, Yellowtail Snappers, a Spotted Trunkfish, Green Moray Eels and even an orange Seahorse. The recommended maximum diving depth is 100 feet. Good snorkeling value when the sea is calm.

Boats with divers are a daily returning spectacle on Bonaire

38. La Dania's Leap
In terms of reef structure this is one of the more sensational sites of Bonaire. It is a boat dive and suited for divers of all levels. The drop-off is at 30 feet depth and on both sides of the mooring are beautiful vertical walls. Just above the drop-off the shallow terrace has lush Gorgonians. More shallow there is mainly a rubble bottom. The reef slope becomes gradually steeper from 30 feet down, until it gets vertical at about 83 feet down to a depth of 110 to 120 feet. The left side (to the east) of the steep slope consists of a series of valleys and buttresses. The vertical wall is covered with Gorgonians, Sheet Coral, Black Wire Coral, abundant small Black Corals, flat Sheet Coral and Scroll Coral. Going west (right, facing the sea) is another steep wall. This wall is deeper than the one east of the mooring. It is very much like the other wall. Fish life includes Snappers and Groupers. On the shallow terrace you will find numerous Parrotfish and Goatfish. The recommended maximum diving depth is 110 feet. Limited snorkeling value.

39. Karpata
This is a boat or shore dive and suited for divers of all levels. The drop-off is 167 feet offshore and starts at 30 to 33 feet depth. From the shore you enter through a narrow canal in the Elkhorn Coral. The shallow terrace is narrow and almost barren until 17 feet depth. Near the drop-off is a community of Mountainous Star Coral and Gorgonians. The reef slope on the other hand, has a very high coral cover

and is extremely diverse. Large towers of Mountainous Star Coral, Giant Brain Coral, lush Gorgonians, Black Coral and a large variety of Sponges decorate the upper reef slope. The most beautiful part is between 30 and 70 feet depth. Here you can also see some old anchors. Karpata used to be a plantation house where ships came to anchor to load plantation products. Now it serves as the headquarters of the Stinapa (Netherlands Antilles National Parks Foundations) and also functions as a research station. Fish life includes many Yellowtail Snappers, Black Durgons, Tiger Groupers and Yellowmouth Groupers. You may also find here Ocean Triggerfish, Horse-eye Jacks and an occasional small Marbled Grouper or a large Yellowfin Grouper. The recommended maximum diving depth is 100 feet. Limited snorkeling value.

40. Nukove (Doblet)

This is a shore dive and suited for divers of all levels. The drop-off is 300 feet offshore and starts at 33 feet. You enter through a channel in the Elkhorn Coral. After leaving this channel you see some massive heads of Mountainous Star Coral, scattered Elkhorn Coral, Fire Corals. Leaf Coral and Staghorn Coral dominates to a depth of 30 feet. This shallow terrace is very beautiful. It is also a good spot for snorkeling. In the drop-off zone and along the upper reef slope are large towers of Mountainous Star Coral. Buttresses are found to the south. There are Gorgonians, Sponges and abundant Black Coral. The lower reefslope is dominated with Sheet Coral and Scroll Coral. Fish life includes big Barracuda, Tiger Groupers, Yellowmouth Groupers, Bar Jacks, Creole Wrasses, Black Durgons, Yellowtail Snappers, Schoolmasters, Scrawled Filefish and many more. The recommended maximum diving depth is 90 feet. Very good snorkeling value!

41. Boca Slagbaai

This is a shore or boat dive and because of the surf and the long swim only suited for experienced divers. The drop-off is 476 feet offshore (beware: there is a strong current) at a depth of 30 to 33 feet. You can choose out of two dives here: Slagbaai to Wayaka and Slagbaai-south. For the Slagbaai to Wayaka dive enter in the central-right part of the bay and snorkel out to the right. At a depth of 15 to 17 feet you will see six cannon, concrete replicas, which where put there in 1974 for the shooting of the film 'Treasure Shark'. When you reach the drop-off, you start your dive. First the coral mortality is high, but the reef slope becomes eventually more attractive. You will see very protruding buttresses, alternating by deeply cut valleys. The buttresses are quite impressive. Return shallow over a field of Staghorn Coral. Near Slagbaai large heads of Mountainous Star Coral, Leaf Coral, Club Finger Coral and Elkhorn Coral are common. For the Slagbaai-south dive you must enter in the left corner of the bay. Keep close to the cliff and to the left and you will see two real cannon. Snorkel from here to the drop-off, going south-west. You will pass a coral community of Leaf Coral, Club Finger Coral and Mountainous Star Coral. Near the drop-off you will see massive heads of Mountainous Star Coral. The upper reef slope has large coral structures. Coral cover is low on the lower slope. To the south (left) the slope is very steep with abundant Cavernous Star Coral. Return shallow at 30 feet or less. The reef above the drop-off is very nice with a dense cover of Mountainous Star Coral. Fish life includes big Tiger Groupers, Yellowmouth Grouper, Barracuda, Schoolmaster, Horse-eye Jack, Nassau Grouper, Black Durgons and many more. The recommended maximum diving depth is 90 feet for both dives. Good snorkeling value, especially if you go north, right facing the sea

42. Playa Funchi

This is a shore dive and suited for divers of all levels. This beach is a popular snorkeling sport among visitors of the Washington-Slagbaai National Park. The drop-off is 430 feet offshore at a depth of 37 to 40 feet. The shallow terrace is wide and shows an extensive field of Staghorn Coral in the center of the bay. Close to the drop-off is a narrow zone with Mountainous Star Coral and also on the upper reef slope this coral is present. The reef slope is varied, but has no distinct zonation. Sponges and Pinnate Black Coral are present. Return (to the south) back into the bay above the drop-off and you will see a very pretty coral community of Mountainous Star Coral, Fire Corals, Leaf Coral and Yellow Pencil Coral. To the north the reef slope is initially similar to the south, but gradually more Gorgonians appear and coral mortality is higher. Return again shallow. Just above the drop-off Mountainous Star Coral isdominant. Towards the shore you will see Staghorn Coral and Pillar Coral, and further inshore Leaf Coral, Fire Corals, Smooth Brain Coral and Elkhorn Coral. Fish life includes abundant Creole Wrasses, Creole Fish, Yellowtail Snappers and Schoolmasters. Here you may also see large Bar Jacks, Ocean Triggerfish, Yellowfin Groupers, a Nassau Groupers, big Rock Hinds, Whitespotted Filefish, Midnight Parrotfish, French

Angelfish and a Southern Stingray.
The recommended maximum diving depth is 90 feet. The north side of the bay offers good snorkeling value.

43. Playa Bengé
This is a shore dive and because of the rough entry and the possibility of current only suited for experienced divers. The drop-off is 400 feet offshore at 33 feet depth. Enter the water in the center of the bay and swim out almost perpendicular to the beach. On the shallow terrace to the north you will see Elkhorn Coral, Brain Coral, Fire Corals, Encrusting Colonial Anemones, Common Sea Fans and Leaf Coral. Amongst the fishes, that are abundant you will see the Jewelfish, Sergeant Majors, Redlip Blennies, Brown Chromis, Bluestriped Grunts, Mahogany Snappers, Glassy Sweepers and some big Tiger Groupers. Do not be surprised to find a resting Nurse Shark here. When you reach the drop-off, you will see that the upper reef slope is covered with Mountainous Star Coral, Giant Brain Coral and Deepwater Gorgonians. At 83 feet is a sand terrace, followed by a second drop-off. Further north the sand terrace is at 110 feet. The sand terrace narrows and becomes continuous with the reef slope that is getting steeper. If you follow the slope down to 133 feet you will see a vertical wall. This wall goes down to 160 feet and it is covered with Purple Tube Sponges, Tub Sponges, Yellow Sponges and White Sponges, Deepwater Gorgonians, Black Wire Corals and many more. The underwater fauna is very spectacular. Return shallow where there be no current. The recommended maximum diving depth is 150 feet. Very good snorkeling value as well.

44. Boca Bartól
This is a shore dive and because of the difficult surf, rough entry and currents this dive is only suited for highly experienced divers. The drop-off is 500 feet offshore and starts at 37 to 40 feet. Two dives are possible here: a northern deep dive of 160 feet and a less deep dive southward of about 80 feet depth. In both cases it is wise to dive with an experienced dive guide who is familiar with this dive site. The underwater flora and fauna here are outright fantastic, but as said before, this dive site is only suited for highly experienced divers. When the sea is calm, this site offers good snorkeling value.
In the future the number of dive sites on Bonaire will be increased with about thirty places. This is an initiative of Captain Don Stewart, who has been living on the island for 25 years and is the nestor of the diving sport on Bonaire. For

up-to-date information about these new dive sites, contact the various dive operations or the Bonaire Tourist Board Office atKralendijk.

SAILING

There are also possibilities to make a sailing trip or to rent a sailing boat. Just as for surfing the weather conditions for sailing are ideal. For an organized sailing trip apply to Dive Inn, Kaya C.E.B. Hellmund 27, tel. 8761. A half day sailing trip with the Iltshi from 10.00 a.m. to 02.00 p.m. costs $ 20.- per person and a whole day trip from 10.00 a.m. to 4.00 p.m. costs $ 35.- per person (including sandwiches and soft drinks). There is a stop on Klein Bonaire for lunch, swimming and snorkeling. A Sunset-trip from 5.00 to 7.00 p.m. costs $ 15.- per person (including rum punch). A sailing trip with barbecue on Klein Bonaire costs $ 25.- (including barbecue, drinks, etc.) per person (you may take diving equipment with you). At the Bonaire Scuba Center at the Bonaire Beach Hotel (tel. 8978) a Sunset Cruise costs $ 13.- a person.
If you want to sail yourself, you would have to rent a small sailing vessel - a Sunfish. Apply to Dive Inn, Kaya C.E.B. Hellmund 27, tel. 8761. Here you pay for a Sunfish, which can hold maximally 2 persons, $ 8.- per hour or $ 60.- per 10 hours. At Ocean Breeze Watersports, on the beach near the Bonaire Beach Hotel (tel. 8978) you pay for a Sunfish: $ 20.- per half hour and $ 30.- per hour.

SNORKELING

The Caribbean Sea is as clear as glass, the temperature of the water is pleasant and the underwater world is magnificent. If you like snorkeling, this is the right place for you. The dive operations and tour operators do not organize special snorkel trips, but it is possible to join one of the many boats with divers, sailing daily. Inquire at the dive center of your hotel or apartment for more detailed information. A number of snorkel places can also be reached over land and by car. Below a survey of the most beautiful snorkel places. Of the 44 dive sites pointed out by the Stinapa (see Major Dive Sites) the following offer good snorkeling value: Pink Beach (no. 3), Windsock Steep (no. 9), Town Pier (no. 11), Just-a-nice-dive (no. 12), Twixt (no. 18), Valerie's Hill (no. 19), Mi Dushi (no. 20), Jerry's Jam/Ebo's Special (no. 22), Leonora's Reef (no. 23), Knife (no. 24), Sampler (no. 25), No Name (no. 26), La Machaca (no. 30), Cliff (no. 31), Petries Pillar (no. 33), Nukove (no. 40), Playa Funchi (no. 42) and Playa Bengé (no. 43). According to experts the best snorkel places of the island are: Jerry's Jam/Ebo's Special, Knife, La Machaca, Cliff, Nukove and Playa Bengé. On these places non-divers can get acquainted with the very fascinating underwater world of Bonaire. Take care you do not get sunburnt; when the sun is high and you are in salt water, it is wiser to protect your back by putting on a T-shirt.

SPEEDBOAT SAILING

Dashing over the Caribbean Sea by speedboat. At Karel Watersports, Kaya J.N.E. Craane, Kralendijk (tel. 8434) you can rent a small speedboat at $ 15.- per half hour.

SWIMMING

Wherever you are staying on Bonaire, the sea is always close at hand and nothing is more pleasant than taking a fresh dive into the azure-blue sea in the morning. If you do not like salt seawater, then the two big hotels - the Bonaire Beach Hotel and the Flamingo Beach Hotel - have a fresh-water swimming pool in which you can have your swim. So at every hour of the day (and night) you can go swimming. However, a warning is due: never go swimming on the rough north-east side of the island. Because of its currents and force the sea is not reliable there and swimming peri-lous! If you want to sun (again) after swimming, especially do not forget during the first days to put some (more) sun lo-tion onto your skin, for the sun is very fierce and the combi-nation of salt and water on your skin intensify its effect.

TENNIS

Of the hotels the Bonaire Beach Hotel and the Flamingo Beach Hotel each have a tennis court. Hotel guests can use this court free of charge. Rackets as well as balls are freely available for the guests. Non-guests of the Bonaire Beach Hotel pay Naf 10.- per hour. In Kralendijk there are two other tennis courts. These belong to the Bonaire Tennisclub. Guests of the Flamingo Beach Hotel can use these courts free of charge. Otherwise you have to pay Na*f* 7.50 per hour and in the evening Na*f* 4.50 per hour extra for the lighting. On Saturday morning between 9.00 and 12.00 a.m. tennis lessons are given on these courts. The courts are open all week until 1.00 at night at the latest. For bookings, payments and information apply to the Kaya Manuel Piar 5. Do not expect gravel or grass courts here, but concrete courts. They are illuminated so that it is also possible to play tennis in the evening. In practice this will happen more often, for in daytime the temperature is rising to a level that does not make playing tennis really recommendable. If nevertheless you go and play tennis in daytime, watch out you do not get sunburnt. Wearing a cap is therefore recommended.

WATER SKIING

There is a limited possibility for water skiing. Here are some addresses to which you can apply. At Dive Inn, Kaya C.E.B. Hellmund 27 (tel. 8761) you can mono- or double-waterski, per hour: $ 30.--, per half hour: $ 20.-. Further you can waterski at the Bonaire Scuba Center, at Bonaire Beach Hotel (tel. 8978). Here you pay $ 15.- for 15 minutes. At this same hotel is also Oceanbreeze Watersports (tel. 8978). Here you pay for half an hour waterskiing $ 20.- and for one hour $ 30.-.

WINDSURFING

A sport that has become very popular in a short time and for which Bonaire is also a lovely place. This is not surprising for the conditions are simply ideal: the fine weather, a magnificent sea and a steadily blowing tradewind (averaging 16 knots) make Bonaire a favorite place for surfers. At various addresses you may rent surfboards or get surf lessons. At OceanbreezeWatersports on the beach near the Bonaire Beach Hotel (tel. 8978) you can follow a windsurfing course. Per hour $ 15.- and per 4 hours $ 40.-. You can also rent Mistral surfboards here at $ 8.- per hour or $ 60.- per 10 hours (deposit: $ 30.-). At Dive Inn, Kaya C.E.B. Hellmund, Kralendijk (tel. 8761) you can rent a surfboard as well at $ 8.- per hour.

The main street - Kaya Grandi - of Kralendijk

SHOPPING

Usually the shops on Bonaire are open from 8.00 a.m. - 6.00 p.m. A number of shops closes from 12.00 - 2.00 p.m. On Sundays most shops are closed. If cruise-ships call at the harbor, some shops may open on Sundays and public holidays in the morning. If you want to go shopping 'large-scale', you would have to make a daytrip to Aruba or Curaçao. On these islands you can purchase articles from all over the world. Often at very sharp prices. Perfumes, jewelry, watches, cameras, crystal, crockery, liquor, brand-wear and many more fine and especially luxury goods. Besides, locally made souvenirs are obtainable. Bonaire may not be a shopping paradise as, for instance, nearby Curaçao, yet you can buy nice things here. Below a survey of the most important shops of Bonaire that are worth visiting. The question is of course what you are looking for, therefore the shops have been arranged per type/sort. Highly recommended are The Home Collection Shop and The Birds of Paradise Boutique at the Bonaire Shopping Gallery.

Beauty Salon
Krisly, Kaya Grandi 69, Kralendijk
Daniella, Kaya J.N.E. Craane 38, Kralendijk

Bijoux/Accessories
Birds of Paradise Boutique, Bonaire Shopping Gallery, Kralendijk

Book Shops
Bonaire Book & Gift Shop (De Wit), Kaya Grandi 50, Kralendijk
El Chico, Kaya Grandi 42, Kralendijk
Home Collection Shop, Bonaire Shopping Gallery, Kralendijk
St Augustinus, Kaya Grandi 21, Kralendijk

Chemist's/Pharmacy
Botica Bonaire, Kaya Grandi 27, Kralendijk
Cambes, Kaya Grandi 41, Kralendijk
Casa Pana, Kaya Grandi 5, Kralendijk
La Linda, Kaya L.D. Gerharts 18, Kralendijk
Novelty Shop, Kaya Grandi 32, Kralendijk

Children's clothing
Pitufo, Kaya L.D. Gerharts, Kralendijk

Chinaware/Crystal
Home Collection Shop, Bonaire Shopping Gallery, Kralendijk
Littman Jewelers, Kaya Grandi 33, Kralendijk
Spritzer & Fuhrmann, Kaya Grandi 29, Kralendijk
Computer
Caribe Automated & Co., Kaya Prinses Marie 12, Kralendijk

Delicatessen
Ariës Boutique, Kaya Grandi 35, Kralendijk
Delicatessen Panaderia, Pastleria, Fruteria, Kaya L.D. Gerharts 7, Kralendijk
Supermarket Jenny's, Kaya Grandi 49-51, Kralendijk
Cultimara, Kaya L.D. Gerharts, Kralendijk

Electronics
Boolchand's, Kaya Grandi 19 and 52, Kralendijk
Casa Nena N.V., Kaya Simon Bolivar, Kralendijk
Inpo N.V., Kaya Grandi, Kralendijk
Kralendijk Agencies & Sales N.V., Kaya Grandi 38C, Kralendijk
Winkel & Zonen, Kaya Grandi 23, Kralendijk

Jewelry
Littman Jewelers, Kaya Grandi 23, Kralendijk
Spritzer & Fuhrmann, Kaya Grandi 29, Kralendijk

Ladies' and Men's Wear
Ariës Boutique, Kaya Grandi 35, Kralendijk
Boolchand's, Kaya Grandi 19 and 52, Kralendijk
Birds of Paradise Boutique, Bonaire Shopping Gallery
(behind E WoWo), Kralendijk
Boutique Vita, Kaya Grandi 16, Kralendijk
Cambes, Kaya Grandi 41, Kralendijk
Caro's Boutique, Kaya Grandi 34, Kralendijk
Casa Chartina, Kaya Prinses Marie 12A-B, Kralendijk
Centro, Kaya Grandi 37, Kralendijk
Chicucha Bazar, Kaya Grandi 26, Kralendijk
Ki Bo Ke Pakus Boutique, Flamingo Beach Hotel
La Linda, Kaya L.D. Gerharts 18, Kralendijk
La Sonrisa, Kaya Grandi 11, Kralendijk
Michèle, Kaya Grandi 40, Kralendijk
The Earth Line, Kaya L.D. Gerharts 11, Kralendijk
Topaz Boutique, Kaya Grandi 10, Kralendijk
Vanny's, Bonaire Shopping Gallery, Kralendijk

Linen
Home Collection Shop, Bonaire Shopping Gallery, Kralendijk
La Linda, Kaya L.D. Gerharts 18, Kralendijk

Optician
Optica Antillana, Kaya Grandi 54, Kralendijk

Perfumery
Centro, Kaya Grandi 37, Kralendijk
Chicucha Bazar, Kaya Grandi 26, Kralendijk

Photographic Materials
Heit, Kaya Bonaire 4, Kralendijk
Photo Bonaire (equipment hire), Flamingo Beach Hotel
Sanddollar Dive & Photo, Sanddollar Condominiums
& Beach Club

Photo Developing Service
Heit, Kaya Bonaire 4, Kralendijk
Kodarama, Bonaire Shopping Gallery, Kralendijk
Photo Bonaire, Flamingo Beach Hotel
Sanddollar Dive & Photo, Sanddollar Condominiums
& Beach Club
Vinaco, Kaya Grandi 68, Kralendijk

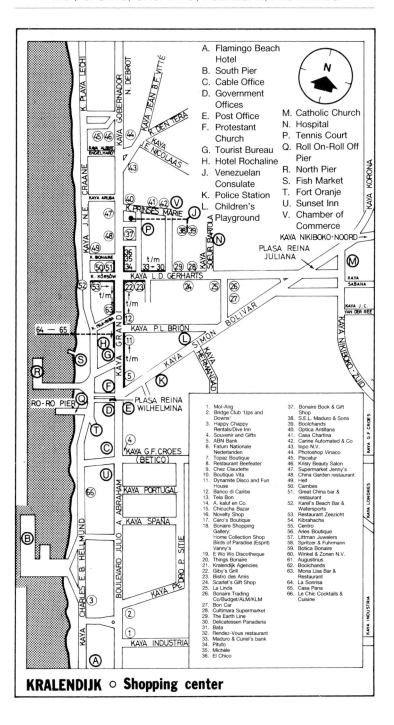

A. Flamingo Beach Hotel
B. South Pier
C. Cable Office
D. Government Offices
E. Post Office
F. Protestant Church
G. Tourist Bureau
H. Hotel Rochaline
J. Venezuelan Consulate
K. Police Station
L. Children's Playground
M. Catholic Church
N. Hospital
P. Tennis Court
Q. Roll On-Roll Off Pier
R. North Pier
S. Fish Market
T. Fort Oranje
U. Sunset Inn
V. Chamber of Commerce

1. Mol-Ang
2. Bridge Club 'Ups and Downs'
3. Happy Chappy Rentals/Dive Inn
4. Souvenir and Gifts
5. ABN Bank
6. Fatum Nationale Nederlanden
7. Topaz Boutique
8. Restaurant Beefeater
9. Chez Claudette
10. Boutique Vita
11. Dynamite Disco and Fun House
12. Banco di Caribe
13. Tela Bon
14. A. kaluf en Co.
15. Chicucha Bazar
16. Novelty Shop
17. Caro's Boutique
18. Bonaire Shopping Gallery:
    Home Collection Shop
    Birds of Paradise (Esprit)
    Vanny's
19. E Wo Wo Discotheque
20. Things Bonaire
21. Kralendijk Agencies
22. Giby's Grill
23. Bistro des Amis
24. Scarlet's Gift Shop
25. La Linda
26. Bonaire Trading Co/Budget/ALM/KLM
27. Bon Car
28. Cultimara Supermarket
29. The Earth Line
30. Delicatessen Panaderia
31. Bata
32. Rendez-Vous restaurant
33. Maduro & Curiel's bank
34. Pitufo
35. Michèle
36. El Chico
37. Bonaire Book & Gift Shop
38. S.E.L. Maduro & Sons
39. Boolchands
40. Optica Antillana
41. Casa Chartina
42. Carine Automated & Co
43. Inpo N.V.
44. Photoshop Vinaco
45. Piscatur
46. Krisly Beauty Salon
47. Supermarket Jenny's
48. China Garden restaurant
49. Heit
50. Cambes
51. Great China bar & restaurant
52. Karel's Beach Bar & Watersports
53. Restaurant Zeezicht
54. Kibrahacha
55. Centro
56. Aries Boutique
57. Littman Juwelers
58. Spritzer & Fuhrmann
59. Botica Bonaire
60. Winkel & Zonen N.V.
61. Augustinus
62. Boolchands
63. Mona Lisa Bar & Restaurant
64. La Sonrisa
65. Casa Pana
66. Le Chic Cocktails & Cuisine

KRALENDIJK ○ **Shopping center**

Record Shop
Dynamite Disco & Fun House, Kaya Grandi 20A, Kralendijk

Shoe Shop
Bata, Kaya L.D. Gerharts 5, Kralendijk
Casa Chartina, Kaya Prinses Marie 12A-B, Kralendijk
The Earth Line, Kaya L.D. Gerharts 11, Kralendijk

Souvenirs
Ariès Boutique, Kaya Grandi 35, Kralendijk
Casa Pana, Kaya Grandi 5, Kralendijk
Heit, Kaya Bonaire 4, Kralendijk
Home Collection Shop, Bonaire Shopping Gallery, Kralendijk
Kibrahacha, Kaya Korsow 1, Kralendijk
La Sonrisa, Kaya Grandi 11, Kralendijk
Scarlet's Gift Shop, Kaya L.D. Gerharts 10, Kralendijk
Souvenir & Gifts, Kaya Grandi 3, Kralendijk
Things Bonaire, Kaya Grandi 38C, Kralendijk

Bazaars
Boolchand's, Kaya Grandi 19 and 52, Kralendijk
Casa Chartina, Kaya Prinses Marie 12A-B, Kralendijk
Casa Pana, Kaya Grandi 5, Kralendijk
Centro, Kaya Grandi 37, Kralendijk
Chicucha Bazar, Kaya Grandi 26, Kralendijk
La Linda, Kaya L.D. Gerharts 18, Kralendijk
La Sonrisa, Kaya Grandi 11, Kralendijk
Tela Bon, Kaya Grandi, Kralendijk

Toys
Bonaire Book & Giftshop (De Wit), Kaya Grandi 50, Kralendijk
Vanny's, Bonaire Shopping Gallery, Kralendijk

Water sport
Dive Inn, Kaya C.E.B. Hellmund 27, Kralendijk
Diveshop Cap'n Don's Habitat
Diveshop Carib Inn, Carib Inn
Diveshop Number 1, Flamingo Beach Hotel, Kralendijk
A. Kaluf & Co., Kaya Grandi, Kralendijk
Sanddollar Dive & Photo, Sanddollar Condominiums & Beach Club

FOLKLORE AND FESTIVITIES

FOLKLORE

Bonaire has a typical folklore, which is maintained at yearly festivities and special performances in hotels. Especially the traditional national feasts such as Mascarada (from New Year's Day till Twelfth Night), Simadan (from the end of February to the end of April), San Juan y San Pedro (on 23, 28 and 29 June) and Barí (from the end of October to the end of December) may be a good introduction to Bonairean folklore (see also under Festivities) through dance, singing, music and costumes. Just as on Aruba and Curaçao, the folklore on this island is the result of the mixing of Caribbean, West European, African, Latin American and North American influences. Especially in the various dances these influences are still manifest. Of African origin are the Tambú and the Tumba. West European influences can be seen in, for instance, the Mazurka, the Waltz, the Polka and the Baile di Sinta. Of Latin American origin are the Danza and the Joropo and Caribbean and international influences can be recognized in the Rumba, the Carioca and the Merengue. These dances are on the programs of many folkloristic events. The Tambú dates back to the slave period and was the only diversion the slaves had after work. Nowadays it is a dance which is danced in particular at the turn of the year and during (harvest) feasts. An important element of the Tambú are the texts that are sung - often improvised on the spot - and in which daily occurrences are being satirized. The name has been derived from the instrument of the same name, a kind of drum consisting of some sort of little cask with a sheep's hide stretched across it, and which is played with the fingers and palms of the hands. The rhythm of this drum is the basis of the dance. Other important rhythm instruments are the Agan and the Chapi, two different types of percussion instrument. The Agan or Heru is a cylinder of about 16 inches length, with a diameter that runs from small to large, and with a slit on top. Often the other side has an iron ring with which the instrument is put around the wrist. The instrument is played with a little stick. The Chapi is a heel used as a percussion instrument. The thumb is put through the hole in the middle and the instrument rests on the fingers. It is then hit with a small iron stick. The basic pattern of the Tambú is two-four time. Besides the tambú player the leading singer, the man or woman, who improvises texts on the rhythm, is also important. These texts employ all sorts of daily events in the lives of the islanders. The dancers do not touch during the dance. Therefore this is a dance which can be danced very well without a partner. In the past fairly frequently the men would start a fight over certain female dancing-partners. These quarrels were fought out with sticks and were only made up when one of the men had sustained a head injury, after which the victor could continue dancing with the woman. Fortunately, these ritual fights about a dancing-partner no longer occur.

The Tumba is a civilized version of the Tambú and therefore closely related to the latter dance. It is also a two-four time dance in two parts (this dance used to consist of two parts of eight steps each) and here as well a leading singer used to improvise texts satirizing the local population. These texts are still an important element of the Tumba, judging by the great number of lyricists who yearly participate in the Tumba-festivals. For that matter, 'tumba' is also the name of an African drum. In the case of the Tumba the drum is not the main instrument, as it is in the Tambú, but only a modest accompanying instrument. The so-called harvest songs also find their origin in Africa. The harvest feast on Bonaire is called Simadan (on Curaçao Seú). Again this is the name of an instrument as well: a kind of tub containing water with a scooped-out calabash floating in it. This calabash is beaten either with two sticks or with the fingers. The Simadan is polyrhythmical and built up in the same way as the Tambú and the Tumba: in two-four time, with two parts and two eight notes. Besides the harvest songs there are also so-called work songs, made up of short periods of eight measures. One distinguishes so-called hammock songs, unloading-songs, filling-in songs and Saturday songs. These songs were especially sung during manual labor in order to make the work go smoother.

As far as dances with European influences are concerned, the pattern and rhythm of the Mazurka are similar to those of the European version. The only difference is that the Antillean version is lavishly embellished. The Waltz on Bonaire is different from the European version because of its rhythmic accents, which seem to create a polyrhythmic effect. Therefore we can certainly call it a typically Antillean Waltz. At the beginning of this century two typical waltz types originated on the Antilles, a waltz in two parts and a waltz in three parts, both without introduction or text. Apart from its characteristic rhythmic patterns the Antillean Waltz is

Beautiful clothing at a folkloristic show

danced to a special rhythm, as only an Antillean can. Have a try during a folkloristic event, it will be harder than you think.... The Polka here is not or hardly different from the European polka.

Caribbean influences can be recognized in the Danza. We distinguish four types: the Danza in one part, the Danza in two parts and the Danza in three parts with an introduction of eight measures (called Chaine: every man gives his right hand to the lady standing left of him, then he moves to the left side of the next lady, turns right around her and gives his right hand to the next lady, etc. until he is back at his own lady again), and the Danza in two parts without this introduction. The three-part Danza is a dance in two-four time. The first part is danced in groups and is derived from the Quadrille, the two other parts are, respectively, slow, legato and lively. The rhythmic basis of this dance is formed by a triole followed by two eight notes, performed in such a way, however, that it seems there are five full counts. In the popular Danza in two parts we recognize in the second part a slow tumba! In the Joropo we find Spanish and African influences. This dance came to Bonaire via Venezuela where it was already popular at the end of the eighteenth century. A lot of barrels of the small typically Antillean Ka'i organ often contain one or more Joropos. For that matter, this Ka'i organ is a very popular instrument on the Antilles. This hand organ originally comes from Europe (Italy) and since the end of last century it has been an integral part of

Antillean folklore. By means of a crank a wooden cylinder is turned round. In this cylinder are tacks, which by means of a percussion mechanism touch the strings, stretched in a vertical soundbox, in such a way that a lovely melody is the result. It is obvious that this result greatly depends on the skill with which the tacks were placed in the cylinder. This is a skill which only few people still have.

The Rumba, the Carioca and the Merengue are not different on Bonaire and are danced in the same way as elsewhere in the world. The Baile di Sinta (a so-called fertility dance) is a group dance of European origin, during which ribbons are wound around a pole to the time of, for instance, the Waltz or the Mazurka (or other Antillean music). It looks simple, but it should not be underestimated. It is quite a feat to 'dance' loose the ribbons without problems after they have been wound around the pole.

A large number of these dances is demonstrated during special performances by folkloristic groups — Grupo Folklóriko — consisting of eight dancers, four men and four women, accompanied by an Antillean music band. Inquire about the show at the reception desk of your hotel or at the Tourist Board Office. It is certainly worth it to watch such a folkloristic performance with dance and music, because both form important parts of the cultural background of the island. At such a performance you will also see the historical costumes, which nowadays are only worn at folkloristic events. Today people wear the same clothes as in nearly all Western countries. With the rise of the oil industry on the Antilles (especially on Aruba and Curaçao) and the world trade involved, the local costumes have gradually been ousted by Western clothing. Until the beginning of this century there surely were local costumes. For women these used to be the Saya Koe Yaki, consisting of a long flared skirt and a short bolero-like jacket. It was made of flowered cotton material, and the material with the so-called Panya di Perpu (purple flowers) design was considered the most fashionable. The skirt was amply flaring, had a lot of pleats and down the front two frills, which resulted in the back of the skirt being longer (reaching to the ground) than the front. Under the skirt a Kamisa or slip of white cotton was worn. Over this the women used to wear one or two starched petticoats, Saya di Abou, resulting in the skirt's standing out wide. The jacket ended above the waist and had long narrow sleeves and a straight, horizontal décolletage, leaving the shoulders almost bare. It was held together with two golden buttons. Out of the seams on both sides of the bolero hung strips of the same material, which might be tied together under the breasts. Under the jacket a vest or camisole of the same material as the slip was worn. Over the bare shoulders a neckerchief or shawl was worn - the Abrigu - often made of wool or silk. The ends of this shawl were put under the jacket - Yaki - and appeared again underneath. The stockings were white or coloured and made of coarse cotton. The footwear consisted of a kind of slippers (their model similar to that of the modern ballet shoe) made of black material. The last important feature was the headscarf. The women had three kinds of headscarfs: a Sunday headscarf with a hanging-down triangular corner (the Punta diScharloo), a headscarf ingeniously arranged and folded into a specific shape, with golden pins and fine embroidery for festive events (the Pètji) and finally an everyday headscarf, made of white linen (the Lensoe, being the popular name for the Lensoe di Madras - called after the place of origin), pleated into a bonnet and with a knot of ribbons at the back. These costumes date from the slave period and were very popular among the female population. Especially by the form of the skirt you can clearly see it was originally meant to be worn during work on the land. When the women were bending forward, the skirt would not trail across the ground because of the shorter front side, and thanks to the longer back the men could not peep under the skirts. For that matter, the men were dressed in a much more simple way. During work the agricultural laborers (and previously the slaves) wore an ample loincloth (Kalambé) made of jute or an old maize flour sack, reaching to the knees and held together around the waist with a narrow leather belt. During festivities the men wore a wide blouse and long trousers of the same material. Around the hips a broad textile band was worn by way of belt. On the head they wore a straw hat. The foot-wear (Sambarko) consisted of self-manufactured sandals, consisting of a piece of tire tied around the feet with small straps. Later they switched to the Venezuelan Alpargata, an open shoe with a thin sole and a colored upper part. These costumes are no longer in vogue and nowadays you only see them at folkloristic events. Fortunately, Bonaire yearly has a number of festivities (see below), in which the original music, dance and music of the island play an important part. Apart from this, nearly every week folkloristic groups give performances in the hotels, so that during your stay you will no doubt have the opportunity to get acquainted with the old ways of dressing, dancing and making music on Bonaire.

FESTIVITIES

Each year Bonaire has a number of public holidays, which may or may not be enlivened by folkloristic activities. Below a survey of returning events that take yearly place.

New Year's Day
The first of January is an official public holiday, announced at midnight by a traditional fireworks that warns the evil spirits to stay away. On New Year's Day there is often a Mascarade procession.

Mascarade
This folkloristic festivity takes place in the first week of January, between New Year's Day and Twelfth Night. Colorful masks are made and certain events are portrayed in a procession. The Mascarade procession usually takes place on New Year's Day and on the first Sunday of the new year. Disguised and masked persons go in procession through the streets, accompanied by a musical group, consisting of a Simfonia di man (literally translated 'hand-accordion'), two guitars, two kuartas, a wiri and a Tambu di dos banda (a double-headed drum).
Carnival
Bonaire celebrates Carnival yearly on a large scale. It is one of the most beautiful events on Bonaire, with parades, colorful costumes, music, songs, dances, etc. Elections (Queen of the Carnival) and contests (best costume, singer, band) are held and the absolute summit is the Grand Parade on the Sunday preceding Ash Wednesday (in 1989 on 5 February). An event not to be missed!

Simadan
This is the Bonairean harvest-festival, starting by the end of February and continuing till the end of April. In former days maize had to be harvested on the various plantations and everyone helped each other. As soon as one plantation had been done, there was a feast and afterwards the people went to the next plantation. During the feasts people danced and special Simadan songs were sung.

Good Friday, Easter
On Bonaire as well these are official public holidays.

Queen's Birthday
Bonaire also celebrates the birthday of the Queen of the

Netherlands yearly on the 30th of April. Besides various official ceremonies, there are also sports tournaments, parades and musical performances. Most shops are closed that day.

First of May
The first of May is an official public holiday on Bonaire.

Ascension Day
An official public holiday, too.

San Juan
Around the holy day of San Juan on 24 June, the feast of St John is celebrated, in which music and dance play an important part. In every residential quarter a fire is built in the evening, which the people dance around or jump across while singing the song Dina Baró. This song tells the story of the young woman Dina who made quite some noise when her slip caught fire when she jumped over the St John's fire. In former days people used to do this to beseech rain and to let the wind, normally blowing hard in this period, subside. Nowadays it is a folkloristic feast. At midnight people go in procession past all houses where someone lives whose name is Juan, Jan, Johan, Juana, etc. Those persons are serenaded and have to stand treat (especially when it is one's birthday that day!). The folk songs connected with this feast are about the saint's life, but also about everyday things and gossip.

San Pedro
On 29 June the feast of Saint Peter is celebrated. This feast is similar to that of San Juan, only in this case people with the names Pedro, Peter, Petrus, Paulus, etc. are visited.
Bonaire Day
An official public holiday on the 6th of September, introduced in 1986. This day was chosen because Bonaire was discovered on 6 September 1499. This public holiday is also called Day of the Flag. The flag of Bonaire is rectangular with diagonal bars in yellow, white and blue. The yellow bar stands for the sun and represents the predominating color of the flora of the island. The white bar stands for freedom and peace, and the blue bar for the sea. In the white bar is a black circle with four arrowheads, which symbolizes a naval compass and Bonaire's bond with the sea. Within the compass is a six-pointed star, telling us that the island population is spread over six traditional villages. The red color stands for blood, a sign of the will to survive.

Barí
Festive period from late October to late December. A lead-ing singer (man or woman) and a choir consisting of men and women sing songs, in which island events are satirized. The vocals consist of questions and answers.

St Nicholas
Bonaire may be far from Spain, Saint Nicholas does not for-get the sweet children of Bonaire. About one week prior to his birthday he arrives with a great number of Black Peters in the harbor of Kralendijk and on the fifth of December all (good!) children get a present.

Christmas
Father Christmas as well is active in these regions: the 25th and 26th of December are official public holidays and there-fore many shops are closed then.

HOTELS

In the hotels many folkloristic activities are organized. These vary from the performance of a Steelband during a barbecue to a spectacular performance of dance groups demonstrating folkloristic dances. Important about these events is of course the dinner that is served. For the most up-to-date information apply to the reception desk of your hotel or to the Bonaire Tourist Board Office, Kaya Grandi 3, Kralendijk. Below a survey of a number of these weekly re-turning shows. The shows marked with an asterisk are in-teresting from a folkloristic point of view.

A La Carte Casino Dinner
Each Wednesday evening there is an à la Carte Casino Din-ner in the Beach Hut of the Bonaire Beach Hotel. Every guest receives free of charge a $ 5.- voucher for the black jack table in the casino. The Duo Cai Cai takes care of the music during dinner.
Start: 7.30 p.m.

Antillean Cowboy Country & Western Night
Every Thursday night Cap'n Don's Habitat & Hamlet organiz-es an Antillean Cowboy Country & Western Night in the bar of this complex. Cap'n Don himself is behind the bar and prepares the cocktails. Start: 9 p.m.

Folkloristic show - Bonairean night - in the Beach Hut

Barbecue Night
Every Thursday night there is a Barbecue Night at $ 15.- a person in the Beach Hut of the Bonaire Beach Hotel, with 'live entertainment' of Chong & Company. Start: 7.30 p.m.

Barbecue Buffet
Every Tuesday night at 7 p.m. begins in Cap'n Don's Habitat & Hamlet the All-you-can-eat barbecue Buffet.

Barbecue Night
Each Saturday night a Barbecue Night takes place at the Sand Dollar Condominium & Beach Club. Start: 6.30 p.m.

Bon Bini Sunset Cruise
Every Monday, Tuesday and Thursday the Bonaire Beach Hotel organizes this pleasant and atmospheric Sunset Cruise along the west coast of Bonaire. For guests of this hotel free of charge, otherwise you have to pay $ 8.- a person. Departure is at 5 p.m. and the cruise lasts approximately two hours.

Bon Bini Barbecue Trip
Every Wednesday and Friday afternoon the Bonaire Beach Hotel organizes a Bon Bini Barbecue trip to Klein Bonaire. Departure is at noon and it costs $ 12.- per person. The trip lasts until about 3.30 p.m.

Bonairean Night *
Every Saturday night in the Beach Hut of the Bonaire Beach Hotel a Bonairean Night takes place with 'live' entertainment by Tipico Bonaireano. On the menu are local dishes and it costs only $ 15.- per person. Immediately afterwards at 9 p.m. there is a Folkloric Show by the folkloristic ensemble Kibra Hacha. This event must absolutely not be missed. Much worth while!

Bonairean Night *
Every Friday night the Sand Dollar Condominium & Beach Club organizes a Bonairean Night with local dishes on the menu. Start: 6.30 p.m.

Champagne Brunch
Each Sunday at noon a Champagne Brunch is held in the Beach Hut of the Bonaire Beach Hotel. The brunch costs $ 12.- a person.

Indonesian Buffet
Every Tuesday night the Flamingo Beach Hotel organizes an Indonesian Buffet with folkloristic dances. Start: 6.00 p.m.

Indonesian Night
Every Tuesday night in the Beach Hut of the Bonaire Beach Hotelan Indonesian Night takes place with 'live' entertainment of the Silver Bullet Steel Band. It costs $ 15.- per person.

Mexican Dinner
Every Thursday night at 7.00 p.m. a Mexican Dinner is organized in Cap'n Don's Habitat & Hamlet with 'live' entertainment.

Roastbeef Buffet
Every Sunday night the Flamingo Beach Hotel organizes a Roastbeef Buffet. Start: 6 p.m.

Seafood Festival
Every Friday night there is an à la carte Seafood Festival with a large variety of fish dishes in the Beach Hut of the Bonaire Beach Hotel. The 'live entertainment' is supplied by The Friends Band. Start: 7.30 p.m.

Seafood Festival
Every Thursday night in the Flamingo Beach Hotel a Sea-

food Festival takes place with 'live music' of a local steel-band. Start at 6.00 p.m.

Steak Night
Every Monday night an à la carte Steak Night with a large variety of meat dishes takes place in the Beach Hut of the Bonaire Beach Hotel. The locally famous Duo Cai Cai takes care of the music. Start: 7.30 p.m.

Sunday Brunch
Every Sunday morning at 11.30 starts the Sunday Brunch in the Flamingo Beach Hotel.

Welcome Barbecue
Every Sunday night there is a Welcome Barbecue with 'live' entertainment of Ayayay in the Beach Hut of the Bonaire Beach Hotel. It costs $ 15.- per person and the start is at 7.30 p.m.

Wine & Cheese Party
Every Friday night at 6.00 p.m. begins in Captain Don's Habitat & Hamlet a Wine & Cheese Party with a presentation of underwater slides.

GOING OUT

Going out and nightlife on Bonaire are limited, but very pleasant. There is a handful of bars and restaurants, on the island, furthermore one nightclub and discotheque, a dance hall and two casinos. Below a survey of the possibilities for going out on Bonaire. Bear in mind that quality is always to be preferred to quantity.

CASINOS

Bonaire has two casinos. They open at about 8.00 in the evening and remain open till the small hours. There is a relaxed atmosphere, there are hardly any obligations with regard to clothing, although bathing suits are not admitted. Just like everywhere else Roulette and Black Jack are by far the most popular casino games, followed by Craps. Popular as well are the many Slot Machines present in all types and sizes. There are penny-, dime- and dollar-machines. So it is possible to gamble modestly. The presence of these machines provide the casinos with a festive appearance and the jingling of the coins always sounds very inviting. As the night advances, it gets more crowded and around midnight the casinos are quite filled and there is a relaxed and pleasant atmosphere. The drinks are offered free to the gamblers and also to the guests playing at the slot machines. Casinos can be found in the following hotels:

BLACK CORAL CASINO
Bonaire Beach Hotel & Casino
P.O. Box 34, Bonaire NA
tel. 8448

FLAMINGO CASINO
Flamingo Beach Hotel & Casino
Kralendijk, Bonaire NA
tel. 8285 or 8485

The Games
Everywhere in the world Roulette is the most popular casino game. The player's chances are always smaller than those of the 'house', but in spite of this it stays a fascinating and especially easy game. If you are lucky, you can earn a lot of money in a short time. If the ball comes down on the number on which is your stake, you will be paid 35 times your stake. In principle you can stake your money in twelve different ways: on one number (profit: 35 times the stake) or on two (17), three (11), four (8), six (5), twelve (2) or 24 (1´) numbers at the same time. The more numbers you choose at the same time, the greater the chance, but the smaller the profit. Besides, you can also stake on red or black, even or odd, high or low. Then the profit is once the stake. As soon as the croupier has said 'Rien ne va plus' or the English version of this, you may not stake any more.

Black Jack is also a favorite game in casinos. A variant of this - the game 'twenty-one' - is played by many people at home. The purpose of this game is simple: you get two cards from the croupier after you have staked money and by possibly buying extra cards, you have to get as close as possible and in any case closer than the croupier, to the 21 points. In principle the cards have the value displayed and the 'pictures', or the jacks, queens and kings are worth 10. The ace counts for one or eleven. The croupier is always obliged to buy an extra card in case he has sixteen points or lower. If you are nearer to the twenty-one points than the croupier, or if he exceeds these ('buys himself to death'), your stake will be paid out. Then you double your stake, if you have Black Jack, viz. an Ace and a Ten, Jack, Queenor King as first two cards, you get paid one and a half times your stake (provided the croupier has not got Black Jack as well, then your stake is maintained). Because of the fact that with Black Jack you can decide for yourself whether or not you buy a card, you can somewhat influence the course of the game. Experienced players 'count' the cards played and calculate their chances in this way. A very complicated procedure not given to the incidental gambler.

Craps is probably the most exciting casino game that exists. It is played with dice and one player throws these on a table with straight sides, while the other players stake on the result of this throw. The number of stake variations is large and demands some knowledge of the game. However, it is certainly worth-while to take a look at a Craps table. If you want to play along straightaway, preferably stake on Pass Line, Don't Pass Line, Come and Don't Come. The quintessence of the Craps game is that the thrower throws 7 or 11 in his first throw. If this is the case, then the thrower wins as well as the players having staked on him (Pass Line). If he throws 2, 3 or 12, he looses. If he throws another number this is called his point-number, if he throws this number again before throwing 7, he wins again. If he throws a 7 before throwing his point-number again, he looses (seven out). In that case his throwing turn is over and then the player to his left gets the dice and the game starts anew. Co-players may moreover bet that the thrower will loose, then they stake on the Don't Pass Line. The Come and Don't Come stakes have the same procedure as the Pass Line and Don't Pass Line stakes, on the understanding that they are staked after a thrower's first throw and therefore imply a choice between the thrower's throwing his point, yes or no.

Slot Machines exist in all types and sizes and are easy to operate: the required coin is put into it and the game can start. Apart from the so-called 'fruit slot machines', the purpose of which is to get three or four similar fruit pictures on a row, there are also black jack machines. Here you play this well-known cards' game with the machine for croupier and poker machines. The offer is much varied and the stakes are in every respect reasonable.

E Wowo, the only discotheque on the island

DISCOTHEQUE/NIGHTCLUB

Dancing is in the Antillean's blood. The big hotels have a room where people can dance at night to the sounds of a local band or music bands. Besides, there is one nightclub and discotheque on the island and furthermore one nice dance hall. The addresses are:

E Wo Wo
Kaya Grandi 38, Kralendijk
tel. 8998

The only real discotheque on Bonaire is housed on the first floor of a beautiful colonial house. At the entrance you see two big eyes on the wall (the name means 'eye' in Papiamentu) and in the discotheque as well a wall is decorated with eyes. Next to the dancefloor is a big bar with stools around it. Furthermore there is a separate room with benches along the walls and a large TV screen. In principle it is a private club, but you may become a temporary member. The entrance is $ 5.-. In high season open every day, in low season only open from Thursday up to and including Sunday. During the week open from 9.00 p.m. to 2.00 a.m. and in the weekend from 10.00 p.m. to 4.00 (sometimes

6.30) a.m. On Sunday there is a matinee from 4.00 to 9.00 p.m. Admission then is Na*f* 2.-. Admission on Sunday night is Na*f* 2.50. In high season there are frequent performances and shows. The admission fee is slightly higher then.

Pirate House
Kaya Curaçao 1, Kralendijk
tel. 8434

During the high season the first floor over restaurant Zeezicht is turned into a cozy restaurant and discotheque/dancefloor. Besides having dinner here, you can also swing to disco music after 11.00 p.m. and occasionally a show is given.

BARS

Finally, attention for some bars where you may have a drink.

Amstel Bar
Kaya Rincón 71, Rincón
tel. 6220

Picturesque bar in Rincón, named after the famous Antillean beer. Simple interior with four tables and a bar with eight stools. Service is friendly. There is a juke box with especially much Spanish music. Not to be missed!

China Garden Bar
Kaya Grandi 17, Kralendijk
tel. 8480

Small bar adjoining the restaurant of the same name. Here you can get take out meals.

Drijfelaar Divers Corner
Kaya C.E.B. Hellmund, Kralendijk
tel. none

Sailors' pub opposite the south pier. Simple interior with a bar with high stools. Open daily from 10.00 a.m. till the small hours. Small snacks are served. Prices are fairly reasonable.

Flamingo Nest
Flamingo Beach Hotel, Kralendijk
tel. 8285

Open-air bar by the sea, part of the Flamingo Beach Hotel. Via a staircase you come to a rectangular bar with in the center the barkeeper. Furthermore, there is a small bar with a popcorn machine and next to it a large terrace with tables and parasols. Happy hour from 5.30 to 6.30 p.m. You will be able to enjoy a nice view of the setting sun here.

Karel's Beach Bar
Kaya Kacichi Grandi, Kralendijk
tel. 8434

Atmospheric bar with every night from 8.30 p.m. 'live' music. The bar has been built on piles in the water and therefore offers a view of the sea on three sides. There is a big rectangular bar with, among other things, a TV and five seats along the sides viewing the sea. At night the sea is illuminated so that you can see all kinds of fish swimming in it. Happy hour from 5.00 to 7.00 p.m. Closed on Monday. Here you may also rent boats and the like. Moreover, in the high season you can have dinner here (the food comes from the restaurant Zeezicht across the road).

Mona Lisa Bar
Kaya Grandi 15, Kralendijk
tel. 8718

Cozy old-time pub, part of the restaurant of the same name, with much wood and a beautiful copper tap with Amstel beer. There is a small menu with snacks, such as omelets, sandwich with egg, various rolls, German rumpsteak, Chili con carne, etc.

Rendez-Vous Bar
Kaya L.D. Gerharts 3, Kralendijk
tel. 8454

Bar of the restaurant of the same name with to the right a big round bar and to the left some tables. On the wall are pictures of the Hilma Hooker, the ship that sunk here a few years ago and now is a beautiful diving destination. Coffee (espresso) is excellent here. Atmospheric background music is played. Especially late at night, after 11.00 p.m., it gets very cozy here.

Zeezicht Bar
Kaya Curaçao 1, Kralendijk
tel. 8434

Bar in the restaurant of the same name. Upstairs there is a dancefloor - 'Pirate House' - where in the high season you can dance.

red		gold	
blue		silver	

Bonaire ~ Coat of Arms

CHAPTER 7

PRACTICAL INFORMATION

AIRLINE COMPANIES

The following airline companies are represented on Bo-
naire:
KLM/ALM, Kaya L.D. Gerharts 22, Kralendijk, tel. 8300 ex-
tensions 220, 221, 222 and 248, daily after 5.30 p.m. and
on Sunday tel. 8301.
ASNA: Air Services Netherlands Antilles (charters), Kaya
P.P. Silië 1, tel. 8859 or 8881.
General information number airport: 8500.

AIRPORT

Bonaire has a modern airport, with the appropriate name of
Flamingo Airport. The runway is 8,100 feet long. The airport
is located on the west coast of the island, a few miles south
of Kralendijk. It has a few simple facilities, including a shop
and restaurant. On departure you have to pay (if over two
years) $ 10.- (Naƒ 18.-) airport tax per person.

AIR ROUTES

There are regular flights to Bonaire via the sister-island
Curaçao from the cities mentioned below:
Amsterdam (KLM); New York (American and Eastern Air-
lines); Miami (ALM, Eastern Airlines); Caracas (KLM, Viasa,
ALM); Aruba & St Maarten (ALM); San Juan - Puerto Rico
(ALM); Guatemala, Quito, Port of Spain & Panama (KLM).

ARMORIAL BEARINGS (COAT OF ARMS)

Just as the National Flag the Coat of Arms of the Netherlands Antilles has been adapted to the new situation after

the Status Aparte of Aruba. By Land's Order of 31 December 1985 a new Coat of Arms was introduced. Now it has five instead of six azure-blue stars in gold. The scutcheon is bordered of gules and covered with the Royal Crown. The heraldic device is Libertate Unanimus and is written in azure-blue Latin letters on a ribbon of gold.

On top the Coat of Arms of Bonaire has a heraldic crown, showing the bond with the Netherlands. The ship's wheel represents the Bonairean, being one of the best sailors of this region. The compass symbolizes the skill and sense of direction of the Bonairean, and the six-pointed star stands for the starry sky which the sailors used to chart the course; at the same time it represents the six traditional residential areas of the island. The blue color of the coat of arms stands for the blue sky and for the Caribbean Sea, which has connected the island with the rest of the world and which plays a major part in the economy of the island.

BANKS AND EXCHANGE OFFICES

Bonaire has a number of banks where you can go for your financial affairs. Opening times differ from bank to bank, but as a rule the following opening times are applicable:
Monday through Friday from 8.30 to 12.00 a.m. and from 2.00 to4.00 p.m. Below, a survey of the banks on Bonaire:
ABN, Kaya Grandi 2, Kralendijk, tel. 8417 or 8429;
Banco de Caribe NV, Kaya Grandi, Kralendijk, tel. 8295;
Maduro & Curiel's Bank NV, Kaya L.D. Gerharts 1, tel. 8420 or 8414 or 8404 or in Rincón, tel. 6266.

BICYCLE AND SCOOTER HIRE

At almost every hotel or apartment complex you may rent a bicycle. The cost is $ 5.- a day. You are obliged to pay a $ 100.- deposit per bicycle. For the rent of scooters you may apply to one of the addresses below:
Happy Chappy Rentals, Dive Inn, Kaya C.E.B. Hellmund 27, Kralendijk, tel. 8761;
Bonaire Motorcycle Rentals, Kaya Gobernabor N. Debrot 28, Kralendijk, tel. 8488;
Budget Rent-A-Car, Kaya L.D. Gerharts 22, Kralendijk, tel. 8300 extension 225, telex.: 1280 BTC NA (airport, tel. 8315 or 8300 ext. 235, and furthermore desks in Flamingo Beach Hotel, tel. 8300 ext. 234 and Bonaire Beach Hotel, tel. 8300 ext. 240).

INFO

A Bonairean in Rincón

The stairway at 1000 Steps

Prices vary from $ 12.- to $ 20.- per day. Inquire about the attractive weekly rates!

CAR DRIVING

On Bonaire traffic keeps to the right and international traffic signs are used. Speed limits are indicated in kilometers per hour. In cities the maximum speed is 40 km/h (25 mph) and outside 60 km/h (38 mph), unless indicated otherwise (sometimes 80 km/h = 50 mph). The distances on the signs are also in kilometers. National and international driver's licenses are valid. Generally speaking, the main roads are paved and in good condition; the other roads are of a lesser quality and take much out of your car. If you intend to drive much on rough terrain, you had better rent a car with four-wheel drive. Always check if there is a spare wheel and its condition. Be extra careful in case of wet weather, because oil rests and dust cause the roads to be even more slippery then. Also watch out for goats running free and in the evening for donkeys (especially in the area between the airport and the saltpans in the south).

CAR HIRING

If you have a valid driver's licence or an international driver's licence, you can rent a car. The minimum age is 21 years (at some car rental firms 23 years and for some types of cars even 26 years). There is (often) unlimited mileage. Prices vary from $ 21.- to $ 61.- a day and $ 130.- to $ 375.- per week. Most cars have an automatic gear and air-conditioning (recommendable!). If you are not paying with a credit card, you may be required to pay a deposit. It is wise to inquire in advance after about the hiring conditions! Below, a survey of addresses where you can rent a car:

AB Car Rental, Flamingo Airport, tel. 8980 or 8667 or 8285 ext. 32 (Flamingo Beach Hotel), telex: AASBO 1915 NA; *Avis Rent-A-Car,* Kaya Grandi 87, Kralendijk, tel. 8888;Budget Rent-A-Car, Kaya L.D. Gerharts, 22, Kralendijk, tel. 8300, ext. 225/229/242, tlx.: 1280 BTC NA, telefax: (5997) 8865 (airport, tel. 8315 or 8300 ext. 235, and furthermore desks in Flamingo Beach Hotel, tel. 8300 ext. 234 and Bonaire Beach Hotel, tel. 8300 ext. 240); *Total Car Rental*, P.O. Box 156, Kralendijk, tel. 8313, telex: *KAYAS* 1281 NA;

Sunray Car Rental, P.O. Box 217, Bonaire, tel. 8600 ext. 34;
Trupial Car Rental, Kaya Grandi 96, tel. 8487.

Some of the car renting firms have a desk in one or more
hotels. If this is not the case then it is often possible to have
the car delivered at your hotel when booking by telephone.
There is also often a representative at the airport, so that
you may rent a car immediately upon arrival. It is recommendable, especially in the high season, to timely - some
weeks before departure - book a car in order to prevent
disappointments.

CASINOS

Bonaire has two casinos where you can try out luck. Apart
from a selection of slot machines, you can play Black Jack,
Roulette, Baccarat, Poker and Craps there. The atmosphere in the casinos is informal and there are no strict demands regarding clothing (of course no bathing suits) and
there are no admission fees. Both casinos open at 8.00
p.m. The players get free drinks. Persons under 18 years
are not admitted. You can find casinos in the following hotels:

Black Coral Casino, Bonaire Beach Hotel, tel. 8448 or
8545;
Flamingo Casino, Flamingo Beach Hotel, tel. 8285.

CHAMBER OF COMMERCE

If you want to do business on Bonaire, you would have to
apply for information to the Chamber of Commerce. The ad-
dress is:
Chamber of Commerce, Kaya Prinses Marie, P.O. Box 52,
Bonaire, tel. 8995.
Furthermore you can apply for information to the Bonaire
Business Association, P.O. Box 83, Kralendijk, Bonaire.
If you want to have more information about the investment
possibilities on the island, please apply to:
Economisch Bestuursbureau Bonaire, c/o Bestuurskantoor,
Bonaire.

Youth center Jong Bonaire with a work of art by Frans Booi in the foreground

CHURCHES AND SERVICES

For more information about church services apply to the churches below.

Roman Catholic
Our Lady of Coromoto, Antriol
St Bernardus Church, Kralendijk
Trans World Radio
Sunday School
United Evangelic Mission: Sunday School
Protestant: United Protestant Church, tel. 8717
Jehovah's Witnesses: Antriol
Adventists: Antriol and Rincón

CINEMA/MOVIES

There are no cinemas on Bonaire. This is due to the rise of the video recorder. There are excellent cable television facilities on the island. A number of hotels has cable TV with no less than 12 channels, including some with 24 hours of movies. In this respect Bonaire is very progressive.

CLIMATE AND BEST TRAVELLING TIME

On Bonaire the sun is always shining and it is always summer. The average year temperature is about 82°F and there is always a cooling tradewind blowing from the east and north-east. There is little difference in temperature between day and night, and the temperature difference between summer and winter is only 2 degrees. In January and February it is coolest, then the average day temperature is over 84°F and at night about 77°G. In September and October it is warmest with average day temperatures of 88°F and night temperatures averaging about 80°F. A day without sunshine is rare on Bonaire. The average rainfall is about 22 inches per year. This rain often falls in the form of short, heavy showers. There are no tropic storms and tornados on Bonaire. All in all on Bonaire it is dry and sunny almost throughout the year. The high season runs from early December till late April (prices are higher then) because many visitors wish to avoid the cold winter months in their own countries, but in principle you can visit Bonaire throughout the year. Most rain falls in the months of October, November and December. In spring, just after the high season in April, May and June, Bonaire is very much worth a visit (especially in view of the price level).

CLOTHES

Be sure to take comfortable clothes with you. Cotton, linen and silk are most suited in this respect. Light-weight and casual wear are preferable. Also take comfortable sandals or shoes with you. Hats are not worn because of the strong tradewinds. Especially do not forget to take along sportswear and a bathing suit. Sunglasses are recommended in view of the bright sunbeams. A jersey or lightweight jacket might be recommendable for the cooler evenings, but often you will not wear these because on Bonaire evening and night temperatures are very pleasant as well. In the rainy season (see Climate and Best Travelling Time) a lightweight raincoat is practical. If you want to go out for dinner in one of the elegant restaurants in the evening, for the gentlemen a jacket with tie and for the ladies a smart dress or skirt is recommended, but not obligatory. After all, you are on vacation. The nightclub and casinos have no strict requirements concerning clothes, as long as you do not try to get in wearing a bathing suit.

INFO

CLOTHES AND SHOES SCHEDULES

If you want to buy clothes or shoes on the island, you will mainly be confronted with American and/or English sizes and sometimes European sizes. Below a survey, so that you can see for yourself whether the clothes of your choice are available in your size.

For her Coats and Dresses

European	36	38	40	42	44	46
American	8	10	12	14	16	18
English	30	32	34	36	38	40

Shoes

European	34	35	36	37	38	39	40
American	$3\frac{1}{2}$	$4\frac{1}{2}$	$5\frac{1}{2}$	6	7	$7\frac{1}{2}$	$8\frac{1}{2}$
English	2	$2\frac{1}{2}$	$3\frac{1}{2}$	4	5	$5\frac{1}{2}$	$6\frac{1}{2}$

Blouses and Jerseys

European	40	42	44	46	48	50	52
American	32	34	36	38	40	42	44
English	34	36	38	40	42	44	46

Socks and Stockings

European	35	36	37	38	39	40	41
English/American	8	$8\frac{1}{2}$	9	$9\frac{1}{2}$	10	$10\frac{1}{2}$	11

For him Suits

European	44	46	48	50	52	54	56
English/American	34	36	38	40	42	44	46

Shoes

European	39	40	41	42	43	44	45
American	6	$6\frac{1}{2}$	$7\frac{1}{2}$	$8\frac{1}{2}$	9	10	11
English	6	$6\frac{1}{2}$	$7\frac{1}{2}$	8	9	10	$10\frac{1}{2}$

Shirts

European	36	37	38	39	40	41	42
English/American	14	$14\frac{1}{2}$	15	$15\frac{1}{2}$	$15\frac{1}{4}$	16	$16\frac{1}{2}$

Socks

European	39	40	41	42	43	44	45
English/European	$9\frac{1}{2}$	10	$10\frac{1}{2}$	11	$11\frac{1}{2}$	12	$12\frac{1}{2}$

The beautiful Playa Lechi

CLUBS

On Bonaire a large number of associations and clubs is active and members from outside Bonaire are always welcome. Below a survey of the most important clubs:

Jaycees, meeting each last Wednesday of the month, tel. 8285;
Kiwanis, meeting every Thursday at 7.00 p.m. in the Bonaire Beach Hotel, tel. 8299;
Lions, each month two meetings, tel. 8546;Rotary, each Wednesday lunch in the Bonaire Beach Hotel, tel. 8448.

CONSULATES

On Bonaire three countries are represented by a consulate. For travelers below a survey of these consulates:
Colombia, Kaya Gobernabor N. Debrot, Kralendijk, tel. 4238;
Spain, Kaya Grandi 17, Kralendijk, tel. 8018;
Venezuela, Kaya Grandi, Kralendijk, tel. 8275.

CREDIT CARDS

The main credit cards, American Express, Diners Club, Eurocard/MasterCard and Visa, are accepted practically everywhere. Proper identification required. Below the addresses of the various credit card organizations on the Netherlands Antilles in case of loss, theft and other financial affairs:
American Express, Hanchi di Snoa 22, Willemstad, Curaçao, tel. 616212 or 616213;
Diners Club, Schottegatweg Oost 215C, Curaçao, tel. 614180 or 614181 (after office hours: tel. 75167 or 615821);
Eurocard/MasterCard, Maduro & Curiel's Bank nv, Plaza Jojo Correa 2-3, Willemstad, Curaçao, tel. 611100;
Eurocard/MasterCard and VISA:
Maduro & Curiel's Bank nv, Kaya L.D. Gerharts 1, Kralendijk, Bonaire, tel. 8420 or 8414 or 8404 or in Rincón, tel. 6266.

CRIME AND THEFT

Bonaire is among the safest places of the world. It is safe to go for a walk at night and the number of thefts and crimes is almost nil. Therefore generally speaking you do not have to worry. Many hotels have a safe, in which you can safely put your passport, tickets, cheques and other valuables. Inquire at the reception desk of your hotel.

CULTURAL EVENTS

In 1956 the Cultureel Centrum Bonaire was founded on Bonaire with the purpose of coordinating and, if necessary, stimulating the cultural activities on the island. The Cultureel Centrum Bonaire runs, for instance, the central library (see Library) on the island, it organizes various courses and all cultural and folkloristic activities on the island. Furthermore it runs the Jeugdhuis Bonaire. For information about cultural events and folkloristic shows apply to the Bonaire Tourist Office, Kaya Grandi 3, Kralendijk, tel. 8322 or 8649.

CURRENCY

On Bonaire the valid currency is the Antillean guilder (Naƒ). It is divided into one hundred cents. There are coins of 1 cent, 2´ cents, 5 cents (the well-known square coin), 10 cents, 25 cents, 1 guilder and 2´ guilders. There are bills with a value of 1, 2´, 5, 10, 25, 50, 100, 250 and 500 guilders. The Antillean guilder follows the dollar rate (1 US $ = Naƒ 1.75). American dollars are accepted almost everywhere, as well as the most important Credit Cards and Traveller's Cheques. At the banks you can change any currency. When exchanging Traveller's Cheques you are sometimes asked to submit a passport (expired no longer than five years), the purchase voucher and/or hotel and room number.

CUSTOMS REGULATIONS

For visitors not intending to stay on the island for more than 24 hours, a valid identity card will do. Every visitor/tourist wishing to stay longer than 24 hours, must have a valid passport, a valid (plane or boat) return or continuing ticket, plus a confirmed hotel-room booking for the period you plan to stay on the island. For a stay of over three months, you have to apply for a residence permit. If you want to work on the islands, you need a work permit.

Cai Cai, the guide of the tourist office

DOMESTIC ANIMALS

It is permitted to take domestic animals with you to Bonaire, provided they are accompanied by a valid health certificate issued by a veterinary surgeon plus a certificate of Rabies vaccination. Domestic animals coming from South or Latin America are not admitted. If you stay in a hotel, make sure in advance whether domestic animals are admitted there. For in most hotels they are not.

DRINKING WATER

The drinking-water on the island is of an excellent quality. There is a modern plant (on the west coast near Hato), where seawater is distilled and purified.

ELECTRICITY

The mains voltage on Bonaire is 127 Volt (50 Hertz). 220 Volt is available as well, but that is reserved for stronger appliances (airconditioning, for instance).

EMERGENCIES

In case of emergency the following telephone numbers might be useful:
Ambulance, tel. 8000
Electricity, tel. 8635
Fire department, tel. 8222 or 8580 (airport)
Hospital, tel. 8900
Police, tel. 8000 or 6222 (Rincón)
Taxi company, tel. 8845
Telegrams, tel. 8305
Water distribution, tel. 8330

EXCURSIONS

For excursions you can apply to the tour operators below. They both organize 'sightseeing tours' throughout the island.
Achie Tours & Transport NV, Kaya Nikiboko Noord 33, tel. 8630;

Bonaire Car Rental & Sightseeing Co. NV, Kaya L.D. Gerharts 22, tel. 8300 ext. 225 or tel. 8300 ext. 235 or tel. 8315 (airport), telex: 1280 BON TRAD and telefax: (5997) 8865.

FORM OF GOVERNMENT

The Netherlands Antilles, consisting of Curaçao, Bonaire, St Maarten, St Eustatius and Saba, form an independent country within the Kingdom of the Netherlands. The islands decide for themselves about their form of government, have their own government and look autonomously after their own affairs, with the exception of foreign affairs and defence. A governor appointed by the queen, represents the government of the country on the islands and in the Netherlands the islands are represented in the Kingdom's government by a minister plenipotentiary. The Netherlands Antilles have a flag and national anthem of their own. The capital is Willemstad on Curaçao.

GUIDES

Two tour operators on Bonaire organize sightseeing tours around the island. You will find them under Excursions. It is also possible to rent a taxi for a certain period of time. For more information, see under Taxis.

HANDICAPPED

There are (limited) facilities for handicapped people. The Flamingo Beach Hotel, however, is very well suited for handicapped people. There are rooms on the ground floor with doors wide enough for wheel chairs, and special bathrooms. The restaurants etc. are also very accessible in this hotel. Furthermore there are special diving courses for the handicapped! Always inquire in advance in order to prevent disappointments!

HOTELS AND ACCOMMODATION

Apart from a number of beautiful hotels (see chapter 4 Hotels) Bonaire also has a reasonable choice of pensions, apartments and houses for rent. For more information you can apply to the address below:

Bonaire Tourist Office, Kaya Grandi 3, Kralendijk, Bonaire, tel. 8322 or 8649.
For addresses abroad see under Tourist Agencies.

LANGUAGE

Dutch is the official language and is taught in schools. Therefore people speak excellent Dutch. However, the spoken language is Papiamentu, a melodious and musical language, originating from a concoction of Spanish, Portuguese, Dutch, French, English and some African. Apart from these two languages, many people on the island often also speak English and Spanish very well. They have an excellent feeling for languages.

LAUNDROMAT

An address where you can wash your clothes yourself:
Magero Laundromat, Stadiumweg, Kralendijk, open from 8.00 to 12.00 a.m. and from 2.00 to 6.00 p.m. Closed on Saturday and Sunday.

LIBRARY

The public library on Bonaire is open: Monday from 2.00 - 6.00 p.m., Tuesday from 8.00 - 12.00 a.m. and from 2.00 - 6.00 p.m., Wednesday from 8.00 - 12.00 a.m. and from 2.00 - 7.00 p.m., Thursday from 8.00 - 12.00 a.m. and from 2.00 - 6.00 p.m., and Friday from 8.00 - 12.00 a.m. and from 2.00 - 5.00 p.m. In the weekend it is closed. Tourists may also borrow books here. In that case, you have to show a valid identity card and give the address where you are staying. Membership is Naf 5.- and furthermore a small amount per book is due. The address is Kaya Simon Bolivar 16 (behind the youth club Jong Bonaire).

LIST OF WORDS

Although nearly everyone on Bonaire speaks fluently English, Dutch and Spanish, below some sentences in Papiamentu which might be useful during your stay.

Bob Bini	Welcome
Kon Ta Bai?	How are you?

Mi Ta Bon	I'm fine
Masha Danki	Many thanks
Bon Día	Good morning
Bon Tardi	Good afternoon
Bon Nochi	Good evening
Mi Dushi	My sweetheart
Mi Ta Gusta Bo Hopi	I like you very much
Mi Ta Stima Bo	I love you
Mi Ta Sali	I'm going out
Ki Bo Ke?	What do you want?
Mi Tin Hamber	I'm hungry
Mi Ta Bai Cas	I'm going home
Mi Ta Bai Den Mi Kamber	I'm going to my room
Mi No Tin Gana	I don't want to
Mi No Ta Loco	I'm not a fool
Mi Tin Poco (Hopi) Placa	I've little (much) money
Mi Ta Sinti Bo Falta	I miss you
Mi N'tin Kuenta Ku Bo	I've nothing to do with you
Kuant'r Tin?	What time is it?
Ta Kén T'ei?	Who's there?
Esaki Ta Di Mi	This is mine
M'a Pèrdè Ariba	I've overslept
Stop Di Hasi Pantomina	Don't act so crazy
Unda Bosonan Ta Bai?	Where are you going?

Counting:

Sero	Zero	Diesdos	Twelve (etc.)
Un	One	Binti	Twenty
Dos	Two	Trinta	Thirty
Tres	Three	Kuarenta	Forty
Kuater	Four	Sinkuenta	Fifty
SinKu	Five	Sesenta	Sixty
Seis	Six	Setenta	Seventy
Shete	Seven	Ochenta	Eighty
Ocho	Eight	Nobenta	Ninety
Nuebe	Nine	Shen	A Hundred
Dies	Ten	Mil	A Thousand
Diesun	Eleven		

LOCATION AND SIZE

Bonaire is the most easterly located of the three Leeward Islands, known as the ABC-islands. The island is located 50 miles north of Venezuela and 30 miles east of Curaçao. It is 24 miles long and 3 to 7 miles wide. The total surface area of the island is 112 square miles. This makes Bonaire (after Curaçao) the one but largest island of the Netherlands Antilles. The capital of Bonaire is Kralendijk. In front of the west coast is Klein Bonaire. This coral isle has a surface area of about 1,500 acres and is not inhabited.

MARRIAGE

You can only get married on Bonaire if both or at least one of the partners is a resident of the island.

MEDICAL PROVISIONS

Bonaire has a small hospital - the San Francisco Hospitaal, Kaya Zuster Bartola, Kralendijk, tel. 8900 - with a good 60 beds. For divers it is good to know it has a recompression tank. Furthermore there are four doctors on the island and three dentists. For minor troubles you may send for the doctor on duty via the reception of your hotel. For major medical treatments you are dependent on the St Elisabeth Hospitaal on Curaçao.

MUSEUMS

At the moment there are no museums on Bonaire. However, the Department of Culture and Education has a collection, consisting of archaeological finds, old furniture, (agricultural) equipment, art works and a beautiful shell collection. It is the intention to set up a museum with these objects in due course. For the time being this collection is to be seen in the office of the department. It is open from Monday through Friday from 8.00 - 12.00 a.m. and from 1.00 - 5.00 p.m. The address is Kaya Sabana 14, tel. 8868.

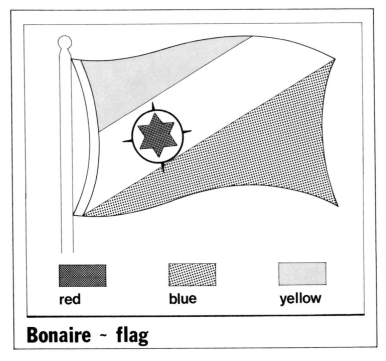

red   blue   yellow

Bonaire ~ flag

NATIONAL ANTHEM

On 11 December 1981 the Island Council of Bonaire officially accepted the following national anthem. The national
anthem of Bonaire has the same melody as the national anthem of the Netherlands Antilles and was composed by
J.B.A. Palm, the text isby Hubert Booi.

Himno Boneriano

Tera di Solo y suave bientu
Patria orguyoso salí foi lamá
Pueblo humilde y semper kontentu
di un kondukta tur parti gabá

Pues larga nos trata tur dia
pa semper nos Boneiru ta mentá
Y pa nos kanta yená di alegría
Dushi Boneiru nos Tera stimá

Larga nos tur ser bon Boneriano
Uni nos kanto y halza nos boz

nos ku ta yunan di un Pueblo sano
semper luchando, konfiando den Dios

Ningun poder lo por kita es firmesa
die stimashon pa nos Boneiru di nos
Y aunke chikitu e tin su grandesa
ku ta halsele ariba tus kos.

NATIONAL FLAG

Since Aruba was given the Status Aparte, the Netherlands
Antilles only consist of five islands. Consequently the national flag of the Netherlands Antilles had to be adjusted. By
Ministerial Order of 20 March 1986 the national flag was
changed, and instead of six stars it now has five stars in the
blue bar. These stars symbolize the five islands in the sea
(blue bar). Apart from a national flag, Bonaire has a flag of
its own. The flag of Bonaire is rectangular with diagonal
bars in the colors yellow, white and blue. The yellow bar
stands for the sun and represents the predominating color
of the flora of the island. The white bar stands for freedom
and peace, and the blue bar for the sea. In the white bar is
a black circle with four arrowheads, denoting a naval compass and symbolizing the bond with the sea. Within the
compass is a six-pointed red star, implying to say that the island population is spread over six traditional villages. The
red color stands for blood, the sign of the wish to survive.

NEWSPAPERS AND MAGAZINES

There are Antillean newspapers in Papiamentu, Dutch and
English. Up-to-date magazines from abroad (mainly American) can be bought on a modest scale.

POLICE

Police headquarters are in Kralendijk on the Kaya Simon
Bolivar. In case of emergency phone: 8000. For general information, the phone number is also 8000. Should you have
had a collision with your rented car, leave the car behind
on the spot and immediately get in touch with the police!
Write down as well the name of the police officer making
the report. Many car renting firms demand this.

Beefeater Restaurant in Kralendijk

POST OFFICE

Post offices are open on workdays from 7.30 - 12.00 a.m. and from 1.30 - 5.00 p.m. The General Post Office is located on the Kaya Grandi in Kralendijk.

PUBLIC HOLIDAYS AND CLOSING OF SHOPS

National public holidays on which the shops are closed: New Year's Day (1 January); Carnival's Monday (Monday before Ash Wednesday); Good Friday; Easter Monday; Queen's Birthday (30 April); 1st of May; Ascension Day; Bonaire Day (6 September); and Christmas Day and Boxing Day (25 and 26 December).

PUBLIC TRANSPORT

There is hardly any public transport on Bonaire. There are bus services between Kralendijk and Rincón and Kralendijk and surrounding quarters, but there is no regular schedule. The only way to travel is by rented car, bike or scooter, and by taxi.

INFO

A boat with divers near Karpata

INFO

Folkloristic costume

RADIO

Various (local) radio stations are active. Many broadcasts are in Dutch. Trans World Radio broadcasts in English, as does Radio Nederland Wereldomroep.

RELIGION

Bonaire is a melting pot of cultures, which is also obvious from the various religions which are professed alongside of each other in freedom and harmony. Whether you are Catholic, Jewish or Protestant, you will find a church of your denomination. Information about services may be obtained from the churches in question or in your hotel (see there).

RESTAURANTS

Bonaire has a limited number of restaurants. For more detailed information see Chapter 5 Food and Drinks.

SERVICE STATION

In Kralendijk on Bonaire is a Shell service station, open from Monday through Saturday from 7.30 a.m. - 9.00 p.m. and on Sunday from 9.00 a.m. - 4.00 p.m.

SHOPPING (OPENING TIMES)

Bonaire has a limited number of shops. As a rule the opening times are from 8.00 a.m. - 6.00 p.m. Some shops are closed between 12.00 and 2.00 p.m. On Sunday most shops are closed. The supermarket Cultimara is open on Sunday from 10.00 a.m. - 2.00 p.m. When cruise-ships are calling at the harbor, some shops also open on Sundays and public holidays during the morning. If you want to go shopping 'large-scale', it is recommendable to plan a daytrip to Aruba or Curaçao. On these islands you can buy articles from all over the world. Often at very keen prices. Perfumes, jewelry, watches, cameras, crystal, crockery, liquor, brand-name wear and many other beautiful and especially luxuryarticles. Apart from this, locally made souvenirs are obtainable.

SISTER ISLANDS

From Bonaire it is possible to pay a visit to the sister-islands Aruba and Curaçao. It is wise to plan and book such a visit in advance. You will be cheaper off then. If you decide on the spot to go to one of these islands, you can buy a ticket at the ALM. Pay attention to the special offers then. As far as hotel accommodations are concerned, there are also special offers. For instance, there is a special offer (two overnight stays in a hotel) to Curaçao under the name of Plan Dushi Kòrsow. In the period 16 April - 15 December you will then pay for two overnight stays - based on a double room - Naƒ 99.- per person. Inquire at the ALM office (tel. 8300) about these special offers.

STAMPS, POSTAL SERVICE, CABLES AND TELEXES

For mailing (picture) postcards and letters the following postal rates apply: on post cards to the US & Canada Naƒ 0.70 and on a letter (depending on the weight, but minimally) Naƒ 1.10. Cables and telexes may be sent via the Landskantoor (Boulevard J.A. Abraham 2, Kralendijk, tel. 8305), which you can phone from 7.00 a.m. - 11.30 p.m. The office is open from Monday through Friday from 8.00 - 12.00 a.m. and from 1.30 - 5.00 p.m. If you stay in one of the bigger hotels, you may of course also send your cables and telexes via the reception desk of the hotel. If you are staying in one of the apartments on the island, this facility is mostly lacking and you will have to phone yourself or call in at the Landskantoor.

TAKING PHOTOS

Bonaire has a beautiful nature, worth-while taking photos of. However, the sharp sunlight requires some precautionary measures. Use an UV-filter or skylight filter. Furthermore, the use of a polarization filter gives extra warmth to color photos and slides. You will get the best results when taking photos late in the afternoon. Film and slide rolls are easily obtainable and you can have colorfilm rolls developed on the island. At some photo shops even within one hour. The quality is good. Slide films as well can be developed on the island. Watch out that exposed films do not get too hot and watch out at the airport when the luggage is X-rayed. In case of doubt it is recommendable to take them home in the hand luggage in a special lead bag. Ask your photographic dealer for further advice. Apart from the photography above water, there are extensive possibilities on Bonaire to take photos under water as well. Whether you dive or just snorkel, it does not matter, for also a few feet beneath the water surface you can take magnificent photos. It is not necessary to have an underwater camera yourself for this purpose, because almost all dive operations rent out this type of camera. For addresses and more information see chapter 6 Diving.

TAXES

There is a room tax of $ 2.30 per person per night and a servicetax charge of 10% (not at all hotels or villas). Airport tax is Naf 18.- ($ 10.-), to be paid on departure (not for children under 2). In case of flying from one island to another (within the Netherlands Antilles, so this does not include flights to Aruba), you have to pay Naf 10.- ($ 5.75) airport tax.

TAXIS (PRICES, TIPS)

On Bonaire the taxis do not have meters and there are fixed prices for certain rides. Taxis can be recognized by the letters 'TX' on the license plate. You will find the fixed prices for instance on a sign near the airport. Some price indications:

Airport   - Kralendijk: $ 5.-
Airport   - Amboina: $ 7.50
Airport   - Flamingo Beach Hotel: $ 4.-
Airport   - Habitat: $ 8.50
Airport   - Bonaire Beach Hotel: $ 8.-
Airport   - Lagun Villas: $ 12.-
Airport   - Nikiboko: $ 7.-
Airport   - North Saliña: $ 7.50
Airport   - Rincón: $ 13.-
Kralendijk   - Lac: $ 15.-
Kralendijk   - Lagoen: $ 17.-
Kralendijk   - Lagun Villas: $ 14.-
Kralendijk   - Rincón: $ 16.-
Kralendijk   - Red Pan: $ 17.-
Kralendijk   - White Pan: $ 15.-

These prices are applicable between 6.00 a.m. and 8.00 p.m. and for four passengers per taxi at the most. For a fifth passenger 5% extra is paid. Between 8.00 and 12.00 p.m. there is an extra charge of 25% and between 12.00 and 6.00 a.m. an extra charge of 50%. It is recommendable to agree in advance about the fare of the ride in order to avoid misunderstandings. Taxi drivers are often good guides in case you want to see something of the island. Tips are not obligatory, but are always appreciated. Taxi company, tel.: 8845.

TELEPHONE (TELEPHONE CALLS FROM AND TO THE USA)

Intercontinental calls (Person to person, Collect Call, Credit Card Call) must be placed through the Overseas Operator, which takes some time. A 30 to 45 minutes' wait in the peak hours is no exception. In order to put in for interinsulaire and international calls, dial: 021. For information dial: 022. Local calls can be dialled directly. On the island itself there are no area code prefixes, so that you can dial the number you want directly from the hotel.

The Bonaire Tourist Office at Kaya Grandi 3 in Kralendijk

TELEVISION

Daily broadcasting from the station Tele-Curaçao (channel 8). Besides, various other channels can be received by cable on the island, for instance, a special news channel (CNN, channel 10), a sports channel (ESPN, channel 3), Venezuelan stations (VeneVision, channel 12, Gala-Vision, channel 6 and Univision, channel 2), Disney Station (The Disney Channel, channel 7), two film stations (Showtime, channel 4 and The Movie Channel, channel5), a scientific station (The Discovery Channel, channel 11) and two American stations (WTBS, channel 9 and USA Network, channel 13). Furthermore, Bonaire has the disposal of Cable television with 12 channels.

TIME DIFFERENCE

Atlantic Standard Time, all year round.

TIPS

Sometimes the tip is included in the bill through a so-called 'service charge' of 10 to 15% - you will find it on the bill. If this is not the case and/or you are very satisfied, you can give an (extra) tip, depending on your appreciation of the service (usually 10 to 20%). In hotels this 'service charge' on the price of room, meals and drinks is always applied. Therefore you should always add 10 to 15% to room prices and prices on menu cards and such, to arrive at the total amount. There is a number of restaurants that do not apply this 'service charge'. So pay attention when giving tips.

TOURIST BOARD OFFICES

For more information apply to the addresses below:
Bonaire Government Tourist Board, Kaya Grandi 3, Kralendijk, Bonaire, tel. 8322 or 8649.
Abroad are the following offices of the Bonaire Tourist Office:
275 Seventh Avenue, 19th floor, New York, USA, tel. 212-242-7707;
815A Queen Street East, Toronto, Ontario, Canada, tel. 416-465-2958;

Torre Maracaibo, Piso 15E, Avenida Libertador, Caracas, Venezuela, tel. 723460 or 723583;
Boulevard Shopping Mall, Oranjestad, Aruba, tel. 33178.

VACCINATIONS

There are no obligatory vaccinations, unless you come from an infected area.

WATER SPORTS

Bonaire is a true paradise for lovers water sports. Surfing, sailing, waterskiing, diving, etc. are all possible here. To the firms and tour operators below you can apply for more information:
Aquaventure Dive Center, P.O. Box 88, Bonaire, tel. 8290, telex: 1926 HAMCO;
Bonaire Scuba Center, P.O. Box 106, Bonaire, tel. 8978, telex: 1291 HOBON;
Buddy's Watersports, P.O. Box 231, Bonaire, tel. 8647 or 8065, telex: 1200 INPO;
Carib Inn Dive Shop, P.O. Box 68, Bonaire, tel. 8819;
Dee Scarr's 'Touch the Sea',P.O. Box 369, Bonaire, tel. 8529;
Peter Hughes Dive Bonaire, Kralendijk, Bonaire,tel. 8285;
The Dive Inn, Kaya C.E.B. Hellmund 27, Bonaire, tel. 8761, telex: 1280 BON TRAD;
Sand Dollar Dive & Photo, P.O. Box 175, Bonaire, tel. 8738.